VIRGINIA CITY

Douglas McDonald

About the Illustrator

Dan Heath has been a commercial artist since receiving his M.A. degree from Cal. State Long Beach. Residing in the Los Angeles area until 1979, Heath then moved to Carson City and opened a shop on the Comstock. Today he operates the Nevada Western Art Gallery in Virginia City's Silver Dollar Hotel, where he resides with his wife and daughter.

 Printed in the U.S.A. ISBN 913814-47-4.

VIRGINIA CITY
AND THE
SILVER REGION of the COMSTOCK LODE

by Douglas McDonald

illustrated by Dan Heath

Published by Stanley Paher

Nevada Publications
Box 15444
Las Vegas, Nevada 89114

Acknowledgments

In putting this history of Virginia City and the Comstock Lode together, I have naturally made use of the knowledge and friendship of several people. First, and foremost, I thank Stanley Paher for his assistance and the use of his extensive photo file. The staff of the Nevada Historical Society and Dorothy Paulsen of the Nevada State Museum were also very generous in assisting my search for photos. Special thanks is extended to Dorothy Nylen and Peter Bandurraga. And, of course, I must thank the people of Virginia City, particularly Katie Kick, Douglas W. Walling, Justice of the Peace Ed Colletti, and particularly Vickie Easter, who has provided encouragement and constructive criticism through the entire process.

Douglas McDonald

About the Author

The three-greats-grandson of Nevada's Governor "Broadhorns" Bradley, Douglas McDonald has been writing about the history of this state since he was 16. At one time employed as the Acting Assistant Director of the Nevada Historical Society, he has also worked as a deputy sheriff in Virginia City, operated his own book store in Elko, and once owned and ran the saloon in the old mining town of Ione. McDonald is the author of two previous books — *Nevada Lost Mines and Buried Treasure* and *Julia Bulette and the Red Light Ladies of Nevada.* He is presently at work on additional books at his home in Silver Springs.

Photo Credits

J. Ross Browne's writings — "Harper's Monthly" October 1860, "A Peep at Washoe" and "Washoe Revisited," 12 bottom, 13, 14 bottom, 15, 26-27 all, 63, 110. Sam Clemens (Mark Twain) *Roughing It,* 68 all, 69.

Dan DeQuille, *The Big Bonanza,* 9, 12 top, 14 top, 56, 57, 60 bottom, 61 bottom, 83 top; Gould & Curry, *Views of the Works,* 20-21 all; "Harper's Weekly" 40, 41, 120 top; Dan Heath art, 10-11, 54-55, 64 top, 65, 95, 97.

Huntington Library, 23 top, 80 top, 118; Library of Congress, 18, 37 top; Eliot Lord, *Comstock Mining and Miners,* 25; Ray McMurry, 91; Nevada State Museum, 23 bottom, 24 top.

Nevada Historical Society, 16, 22 top, 37 bottom, 43 top, 44 all, 46, 48, 49 all, 58, 60 top, 62, 71 all, 73, 75, 77, 83, 96, 103, 105 bottom, 106, 107, 111.

University of California, Bancroft Library, 31, 34-35 all, 36 bottom, 82; Doug Walling, 80 bottom. All other illustrations, photographs and line art are from the private collections of either the author or the publisher.

Table of Contents

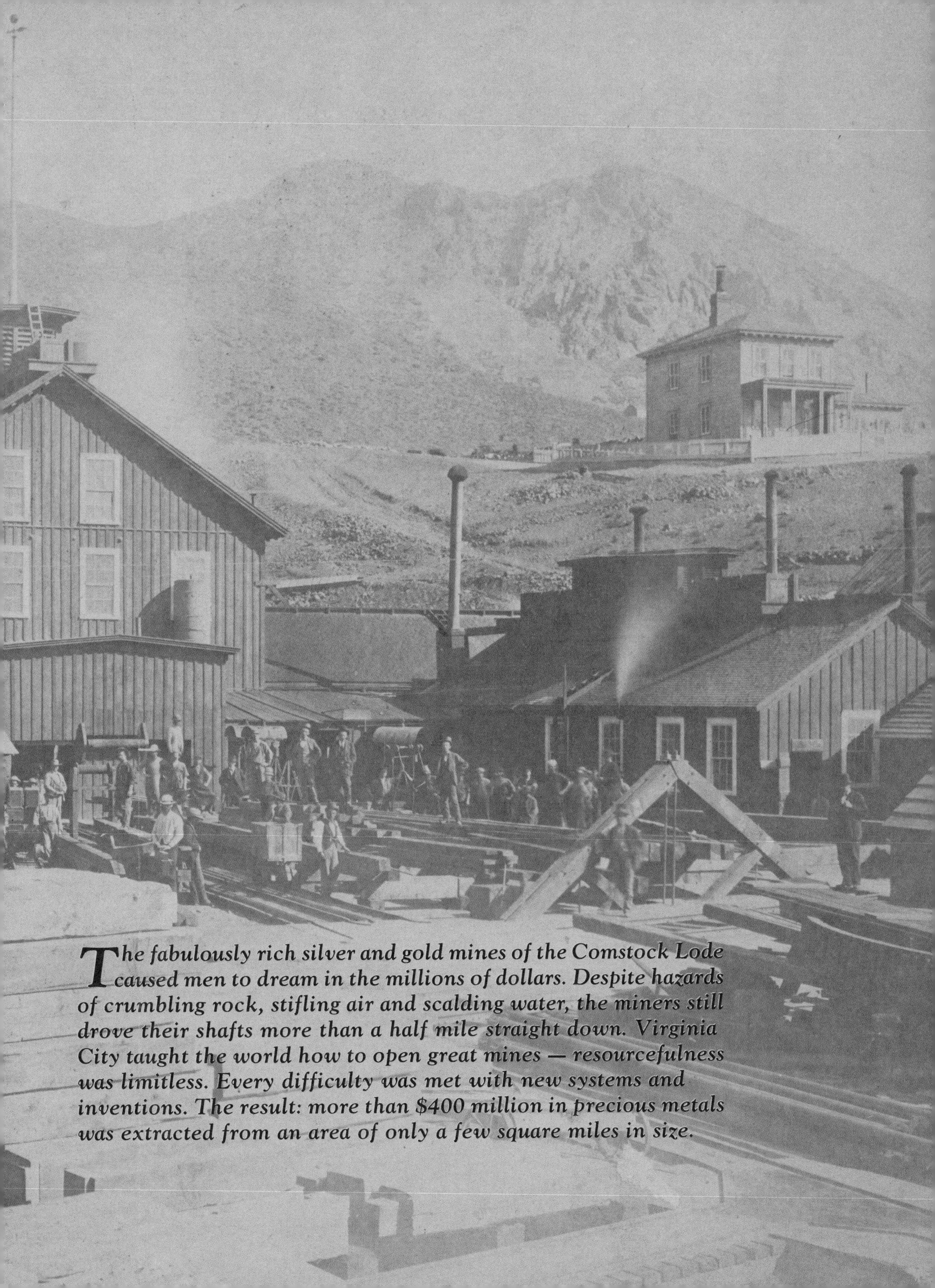

The fabulously rich silver and gold mines of the Comstock Lode caused men to dream in the millions of dollars. Despite hazards of crumbling rock, stifling air and scalding water, the miners still drove their shafts more than a half mile straight down. Virginia City taught the world how to open great mines — resourcefulness was limitless. Every difficulty was met with new systems and inventions. The result: more than $400 million in precious metals was extracted from an area of only a few square miles in size.

The History of the Comstock Lode and Virginia City

Virginia City is situated on top of the famous Comstock Lode, the largest and most important silver deposit in North America. Development of this huge body of silver caused Nevada to become a territory in 1861 and a state three years later, pumping much-needed financing into the federal government while giving President Lincoln additional support in Congress. It was also responsible for the rewriting of U.S. mining law, upheavals in American currency and the world-wide silver market, numerous innovative changes in mining techniques, and was a main contributor in reducing post-Civil War debt. Yet the discovery of this rich lode was a drawn out, practically accidental occurrence.

In the early part of the 19th century, when fur trappers, farmers, and adherents of "Manifest Destiny" were beginning to settle the more productive areas of the West, the arid land now encompassed within the state of Nevada was essentially avoided. In the mid-1840's emigrants enroute to Oregon or California began using trails along the Humboldt, Carson, and Truckee Rivers, but were usually in such a hurry to reach their destinations that they seldom paused along the way.

However, in July, 1849, California-bound Abner Blackburn stopped briefly on the banks of the Carson River. He panned a few bits of gold near the present town of Dayton, but he did not find enough to encourage the members of his Mormon wagon train into pausing here for further exploration.

A year later another wagon train led by Thomas Orr halted near the same spot to wait for the snow to melt in the Sierra passes. William Prouse spent the layover practicing his gold panning technique with a tin milkpan in the gravel of a stream flowing into the river. Much to his surprise bits of gold appeared at the bottom, which he promptly displayed to other members of the train. John Orr and Nicholas Kelly began panning their way up the stream, naming it Gold Creek, until On June 1 they discovered the rock formation now known as Devil's Gate. Here Orr used a butcher's knife to pry off a chunk of rock, thus exposing the first nugget found in what would later become known as the Comstock Lode.

Even though small amounts of gold had been found, the rich placers of California lured the train on when the mountain passes were free of snow. Meanwhile, other emigrant trains had stopped in the vicinity and the success of the young men's panning had become common knowledge. Soon a handful of men were at work placering the lower reaches of Gold Canyon. With pans and sluices they worked from dawn to dusk, recovering at most $5 a day.

A rush did not occur, even though gold had been found in an area previously thought barren. As all supplies had to be freighted over the mountains from California, prices ran as high as $2.50 per sack for flour and $1.00 a pound for potatoes. Housing was crude and barren, often little more than a "dug-out" carved into a hillside. Yet the placer miners worked on, ever hopeful that a large gold deposit similar to California's Mother Lode would be discovered.

A tent trading post was started near the mouth of Gold Canyon, where a small community developed. Called Chinatown for its numbers of Orientals placering in the vicinity, the town would be renamed Dayton after Nevada became a territory.

In 1851, an often-inebriated teamster named James Finney, but known as "Old Virginny," dug his tent into a hillside two miles farther up Gold Canyon to begin mining in that area. Others followed his lead and the community of Johntown was founded, again named for the predominance of "John Chinamen."

To the south and west a small trading and agricultural settlement known as Mormon Station was established. Later renamed Genoa, its farm products soon removed the fear of starvation which faced the Gold Canyon miners in the winter. Little by little the population increased, but the production of the placers remained small, due in part to a curious blue clay which slowed work when it clogged the riffles in the rockers and "long toms."

Two newcomers, Allen and Hosea Grosh, arrived in Gold Canyon in 1853. While their mining ventures in California had been unproductive, the two brothers did know something of chemistry and mineralogy. After spending a year placer mining, they moved on to California, but they had made a

COMSTOCK DISCOVERING SILVER.

Henry Comstock believed that McLaughlin and O'Riley were mining on his "ranch" claim, high on Sun Mountain. This tiny placer operation became the Ophir mine — first on the Comstock Lode.

discovery in Gold Canyon and were determined to pursue it. In 1856 they wrote their father, "We have been trying to get a couple of hundred dollars together for the purpose of making a careful examination of a silver lead in Gold Canyon. Native silver is found in Gold Canyon; it resembles thin sheet-lead broken very fine, and lead the miners suppose it to be."

For awhile in 1856, and again in 1857, the Grosh brothers returned to Gold Canyon. They kept the silver's existence a secret while carefully mapping out ore veins, even calling one "a perfect monster" on account of its size. But without capital to develop the property nothing further could be done, and the brothers were forced to interrupt their studies to pan gold for living expenses.

On August 19, 1857, Hosea accidentally stuck a pick into his foot, creating a serious wound. Adequate medical treatment was nonexistent in the rude surroundings and on September 2 he died of blood poisoning. Allen spent some weeks working to pay off the debts brought about by his brother's illness, thus delaying his trip to California to raise the necessary capital. On November 20 he set out with Richard Bucke to cross the Sierra and immediately encountered snowstorms. They ran out of provisions, killing their sole donkey for food. Freezing, starving, and exhausted, the two men finally stumbled into Last Chance, California, on December 5. With one foot amputated due to frostbite, Bucke survived to eventually become a physician, but Allen Grosh died on the 17th without revealing his discovery.

A year later the Johntown miners began realizing that the placer ground they had been working was about played out. In search of new deposits they prospected in all directions, settling the town of Gold Hill higher in Gold Canyon, and finding color in Six Mile Canyon which led eastward from Sun Mountain. The gold there was lower in fineness but more plentiful, enabling a miner to average from $5 to $12 per day.

Early in 1859 Patrick McLaughlin and Peter O'Riley were placer mining at a tiny spring near the head of the canyon. While digging a small reservoir they found rich, gold-bearing dirt, although it was obviously alloyed with something else as it was colored a very pale yellow. But as soon as word of their discovery got out, they were confronted with trespass charges by Henry Comstock, who stated that they were working ground he had previously claimed as a ranch.

The site was 6,000 feet above sea level on the steep side of a rock-strewn mountain, so his statement was clearly preposterous. Yet instead of disputing it, McLaughlin and O'Riley accepted Comstock and his crony, Emanuel Penrod, as equal partners by giving them 100 "feet" of the seam for their own. A few days

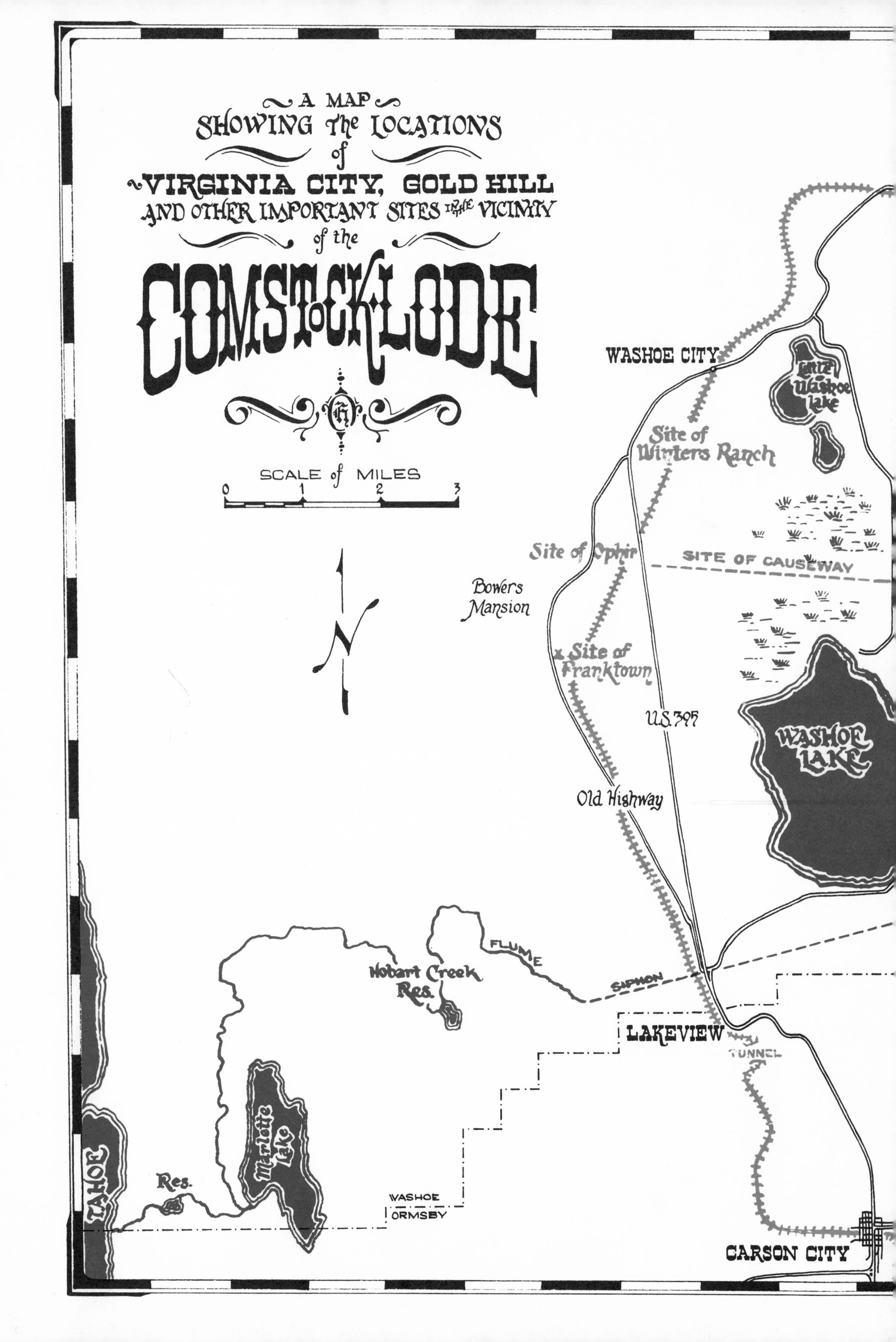

A MAP
SHOWING the LOCATIONS
of
VIRGINIA CITY, GOLD HILL
AND OTHER IMPORTANT SITES IN THE VICINITY
of the
COMSTOCK LODE
SCALE of MILES
0 1 2 3
WASHOE CITY
Little Washoe Lake
Site of Winters Ranch
Site of Ophir
SITE OF CAUSEWAY
Bowers Mansion
Site of Franktown
U.S. 395
WASHOE LAKE
Old Highway
FLUME
Hobart Creek Res.
SIPHON
LAKEVIEW
TUNNEL
Marlette Lake
TAHOE
Res.
WASHOE
ORMSBY
CARSON CITY

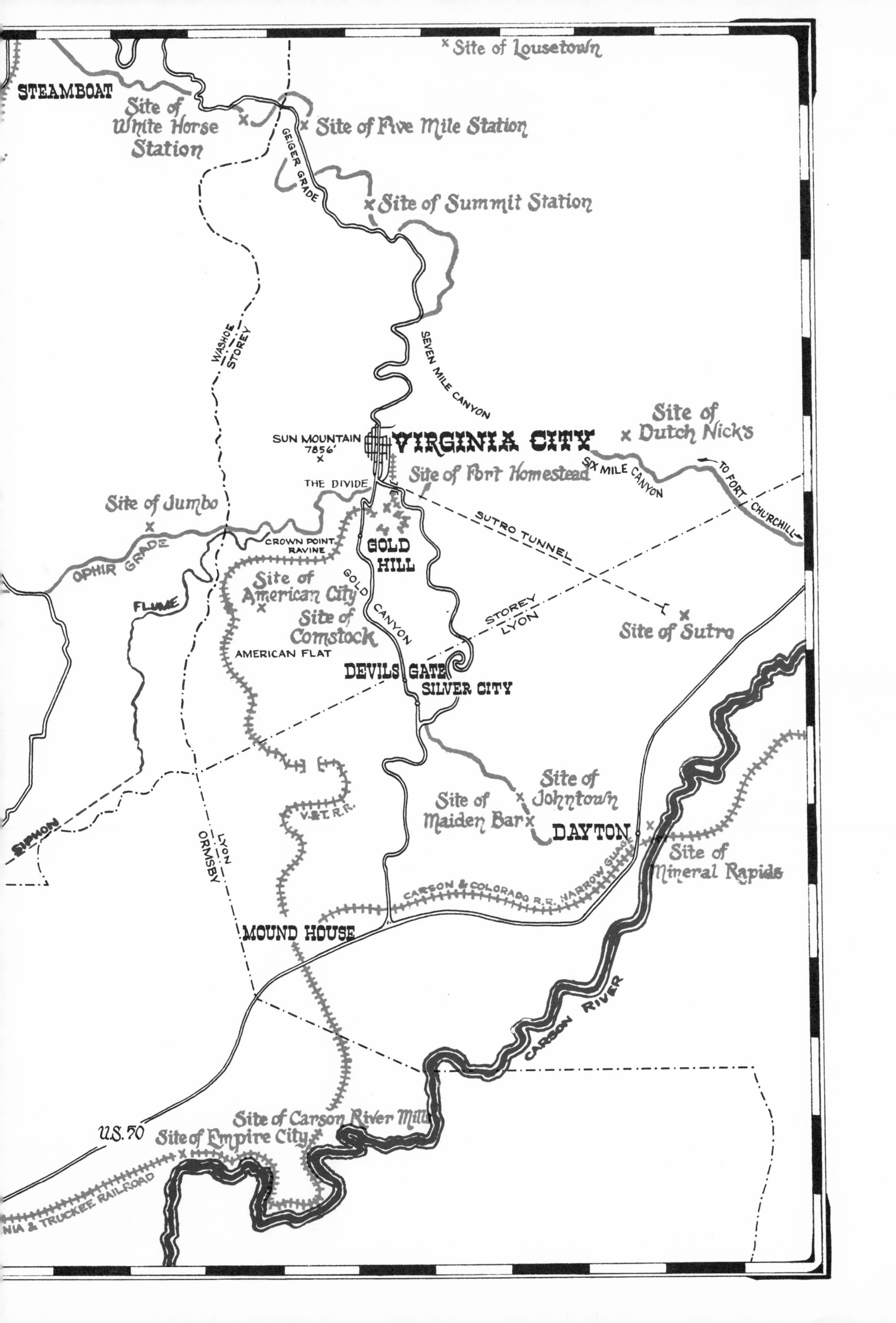

Site of Lousetown
STEAMBOAT
Site of White Horse Station
Site of Five Mile Station
GEIGER GRADE
Site of Summit Station
WASHOE
STOREY
SEVEN MILE CANYON
Site of Dutch Nick's
SUN MOUNTAIN 7856'
VIRGINIA CITY
Site of Fort Homestead
SIX MILE CANYON
TO FORT CHURCHILL
THE DIVIDE
Site of Jumbo
SUTRO TUNNEL
CROWN POINT RAVINE
OPHIR GRADE
GOLD HILL
Site of American City
GOLD CANYON
FLUME
Site of Comstock
STOREY
LYON
Site of Sutro
AMERICAN FLAT
DEVILS GATE
SILVER CITY
Site of Johntown
Site of Maiden Bar
V.&T. R.R.
DAYTON
SIPHON
LYON
ORMSBY
Site of Mineral Rapids
CARSON & COLORADO R.R. NARROW GUAGE
MOUND HOUSE
CARSON RIVER
Site of Carson River Mill
U.S. 50
Site of Empire City
NIA & TRUCKEE RAILROAD

NAMING VIRGINIA CITY.

later local miners met in Gold Hill and drew up the first regulations by which the newly named Washoe mining region would henceforth be governed.

McLaughlin and O'Riley named their claim the Ophir. The four partners were soon joined by two more when Joseph Osborn and John D. Winters were brought in to provide mules and an arrastra for grinding the rock. Work progressed nicely except for a deposit of black rock right in the center of the claim. As the rock was thought to be barren, pieces were given away as souvenirs until June 27, 1859, when a Placerville assayer named Melville Atwood ran a test on one. The rock ran only $876 to the ton in gold but also carried $3,000 a ton in silver. The word spread quickly, sending hundreds of fortune seekers swarming from California to the new diggings on Sun Mountain. The Grosh brothers' secret was finally discovered, the bluish-black clay the miners had been cursing was actually silver, and the "Rush to Washoe" was on.

By November 1, when freighting over the Sierra was halted for the winter, the Ophir had shipped 38 tons of ore to San Francisco. It yielded $112,000 which, after deducting $552 per ton for freighting and reduction, still left an enormous profit of $91,024. Much to the disappointment of those who had hurried to the new strike though, only the Comstock & Penrod, the Corey, the Ophir claims, and the 250-foot Gold Hill tract, yielded any rich ore.

The first arrivals were still determined to stick out the winter, most finding whatever shelter they could on the side of Sun Mountain. A ragged little community developed around the Ophir mine which originally took the name Ophir Diggings. Legend states that the tiny settlement was renamed one night when Old Virginny, a veteran Gold Canyon placer miner, was wending his way home in a highly intoxicated state. He tripped over a rock in the dark and took a heavy fall, breaking the bottle of whiskey he was carrying. Picking up the largest shard, he noticed a small amount of the precious fluid still in the broken hunk of glass. In order not to have broken a full bottle for nothing, he is reported to have poured the last drops out onto the ground and intoned, "I christen this place Virginny Town."

Actually a public meeting was held in September, 1859, where it was decided to name the community Virginia City in honor of Old Virginny's original discovery of the Virginia ledge and the Gold Hill claims. But however it was chosen the name stuck, and Virginia City was born, although the first winter of 1859-60 it certainly did not resemble a city.

Eliot Lord later wrote, "A single street had been laid out in October, 1859, by Herman Camp and Henry de Groot, along the supposed line of the Comstock ledge, running therefore nearly north and south, except when it was necessary to make a detour to avoid cabins whose owners refused to move. On the line of this street two houses of roughly cemented stone had been built, surrounded by straggling lines of flimsy huts. Tents of dirty, ragged canvas pieced out with tattered clothes coated with grime — hovels of pine boards roughly nailed together and pierced by bent and rusty stove-pipes — heaps of broken rocks with shapeless crevices into which men crawled like lizards — shallow pits party covered over with boards and earth — and embryo adits, dark slimy holes into which the melting snow dripped with a monotonous plash — these were the winter homes of the citizens."

MOUNT OPHIR.

While the residents of the Comstock, as the lode was beginning to be called, waited for spring to thaw the ground and bring relief from food shortages and intense cold, other men in California were waiting just as eagerly. Silver ingots cast from Ophir ore had been shown around San Francisco, creating infectious cases of "silver fever" in men from all walks of life. Even before the passes were opened in the spring of 1860, thousands of men began gathering for the drive over the Sierra. Financiers and bankers brought much needed capital, businessmen and traders brought wagons and mules loaded with every type of goods, and countless laborers and miners from nearly every nation began riding or walking over the mountains to the silverland of Washoe. The first trickle to get through paved the way for the horde that followed. Soon the mountain roads became human rivers as men quit their jobs, jumped ship in the harbors, or closed their businesses to join in the stampede.

John Moore was a classic example of one of the businessmen who recognized the profits to be made on the Comstock. On March 9, he left San Francisco with 2,100 pounds of supplies and liquors bound for Virginia City. At Placerville he had to transfer everything from wagons to mules, finally arriving on Sun Mountain on March 31. He immediately set up a 15 by 52-foot tent and laid the area's first carpet on the dirt floor. A partition separated the interior into a bar and sleeping quarters and a U.S. flag flew overhead.

THE GRADE.

GOLD DIGGINGS OF 1859.

It was late in the day before he opened for business but patrons quickly drank up $200 in liquor and 36 of them paid $1 apiece for the privilege of sleeping on the floor in the back room. A few pillows were available, but some had been stuffed with wood shavings on account of the high cost of ticking and a hungry mule train had eaten them.

Everything was inordinately expensive since it had to be freighted from California. By May the mountain road had been somewhat improved but freight outfits were still charging the unheard-of rate of 18¢ per pound. Even so, a traveler in September counted 353 freight wagons, either coming east loaded or going west empty, on the road between Virginia City and Placerville.

Thousands of fortune-seekers descending on Sun Mountain created an awesome scene which Lord described as "the chaotic confusion in which the camp was plunged...a shapeless city traversed by three main lanes styled streets by courtesy. A restless crowd blocked these narrow passages, flowing in and out of their bordering saloons and gambling houses."

Initial confusion over mining rights became enormously magnified as the rush continued. Claims of all shapes and sizes were staked, usually overlaying or overlaid by adjoining claims, and battles were often waged over these boundaries. The validity of many of the original claims were in doubt as well. The record book for the district had been kept on the bar of a local saloon before the rush. There it was available to anyone who desired to make fraudulent changes or erasures, whenever it was not being used as a club in one of the saloon brawls.

Underground it was even worse. The general law for lode mines then followed the old "Mexican Apex" rule, meaning a mine where a vein surfaced, or apexed, had the right to follow that vein wherever it led underground, even onto or through other claims. As the mines went deeper this rule would provoke actual gunbattles before a standard set of mining laws could be dediced upon in the Virginia City courts.

It has been estimated that 10,000 people came to the Comstock in 1860, but less than half that number stayed. Only a few of the mines were producing, there was almost no placer ground available, and all the locations which even hinted at ore were claimed.

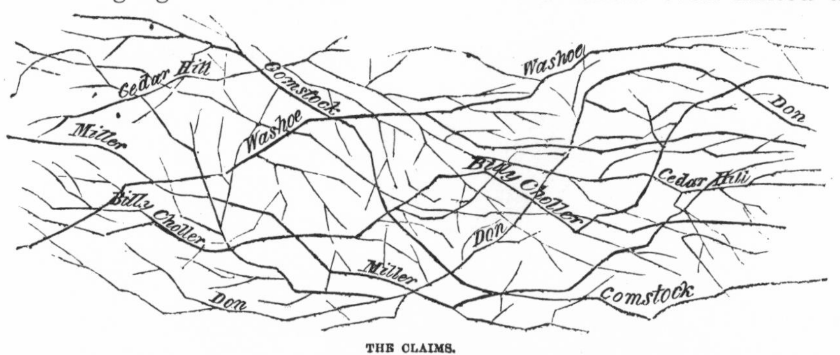

THE CLAIMS.

A QUESTION OF TITLE

Many who were soon disappointed either returned to California or moved on to other newly-founded camps east of the Sierra.

Of those who stayed, most tried to find work in the mines, but swelling clay and heavily fractured ground made underground work dangerous and costly. Perhaps the most famous and useful invention to come out of the Comstock was Philipp Deidesheimer's idea for square set timbering, which was put into practice late in 1860.

Even with improved conditions underground, the mines were still not producing as well as expected. Myron Angel reports a census taken late in 1860 which showed 2,390 persons in Virginia City, only 118 of which were women. A year later the population had only increased to 2,700, indicating that the rush had become stagnant.

Slow as it was, 1861 did bring three changes to the area. Nevada Territory was created out of Utah on March 2, and the location of the capitol at Carson City meant that territorial law was thereafter headquartered only 15 miles from Virginia City. The Civil War also began in the East, producing a flurry of pro-Union sentiment, especially in the volunteer fire companies, causing the creation of military units and posts in the area. The third major change occurred with the construction of numerous stamp mills in Nevada, primarily in Washoe Valley and along the Carson River, to reduce the expense of freighting ore to California for reduction.

The following year things began to improve. Mining stocks that had increased in value so blindly and rapidly early in 1860, only to crash just as quickly, were again being traded. The number of Comstock shares was so great that the San Francisco Stock and Exchange Board, the first exchange in the U.S. devoted to mining stock, was organized. Investors again began pouring money into the silver mines, skyrocketing "feet" in the Ophir to $3,800 apiece and the Gould & Curry to $2,500 each. With added capital, production began to increase as well. The Comstock mines had only yielded $275,000 in 1859; by the end of 1862 that figure had risen to a yearly figure of $6 million.

All of this activity sparked the "Rush of '63," a year of excitement and activity unsurpassed in Comstock history. The population of Virginia City jumped to 15,000, money flowed with abandon, and Comstock society blossomed. Homes and businesses were being built of brick, gas mains were laid, and opulent restaurants were opened. The International hotel on C Street was rebuilt into a luxurious 100-room inn complete with an elevator. More than a hundred saloons and gambling parlors lined the streets but the city also boasted of four churches, three newspapers, public and private schools, and dozens of social clubs or "societies."

But that year also saw the height of violence on the Comstock. Back East the fighting between the Union and the Confederacy was at its bloodiest and this may have contributed to a sudden surge in violent crime in Virginia City during the last half of 1863.

While not directly affected by the violent turn of events on the streets, mining stocks also began to waver. Some major producers which were expected to hit bonanza ore as their workings inched deeper were disappointed to find only pockets of low-grade ore. Others found even their supply of marginal ore beginning to dwindle. By early 1864 a true depression had settled over the region.

Even though the flowery future of the Comstock had dimmed somewhat, it in no way affected the determination of its citizens to aid in having Nevada made a state. The first Constitutional Convention, which had met the previous year, was completely torn apart by conflicts between the Union Party and the Democrats. A second convention which met in July, 1864, succeeded in drafting a totally pro-Union constitution. It was telegraphed to Washington at the exhorbitant cost of $3,416.77 and on October 31, 1864, President Lincoln signed the proclamation which made Nevada the 36th state.

Contrary to popular belief, Nevada was not admitted solely so that the wealth of the Comstock could be used to "save" the Union. Rather, there were three reasons why Nevada's statehood was so eagerly sought. Lincoln needed additional votes in Congress to ensure passage of some of his more controversial proposals, and he wanted the added weight of Nevada's two pro-Union Senators to add to his forces. The President also wanted to strengthen the ties between the Union and the Far West, particularly Nevada with its close proximity to California, to further discourage any hopes the Confederacy might have of gaining a sympathetic movement in the West.

This view of C Street, showing the men and equipment of the Young America Engine Company No. 2 in front of their firehouse in 1862, is one of the earliest known photos of Virginia City. The two U.S. flags flying from the rooftop indicate the fireman's very active support of the Union during the Civil War then raging in the East.

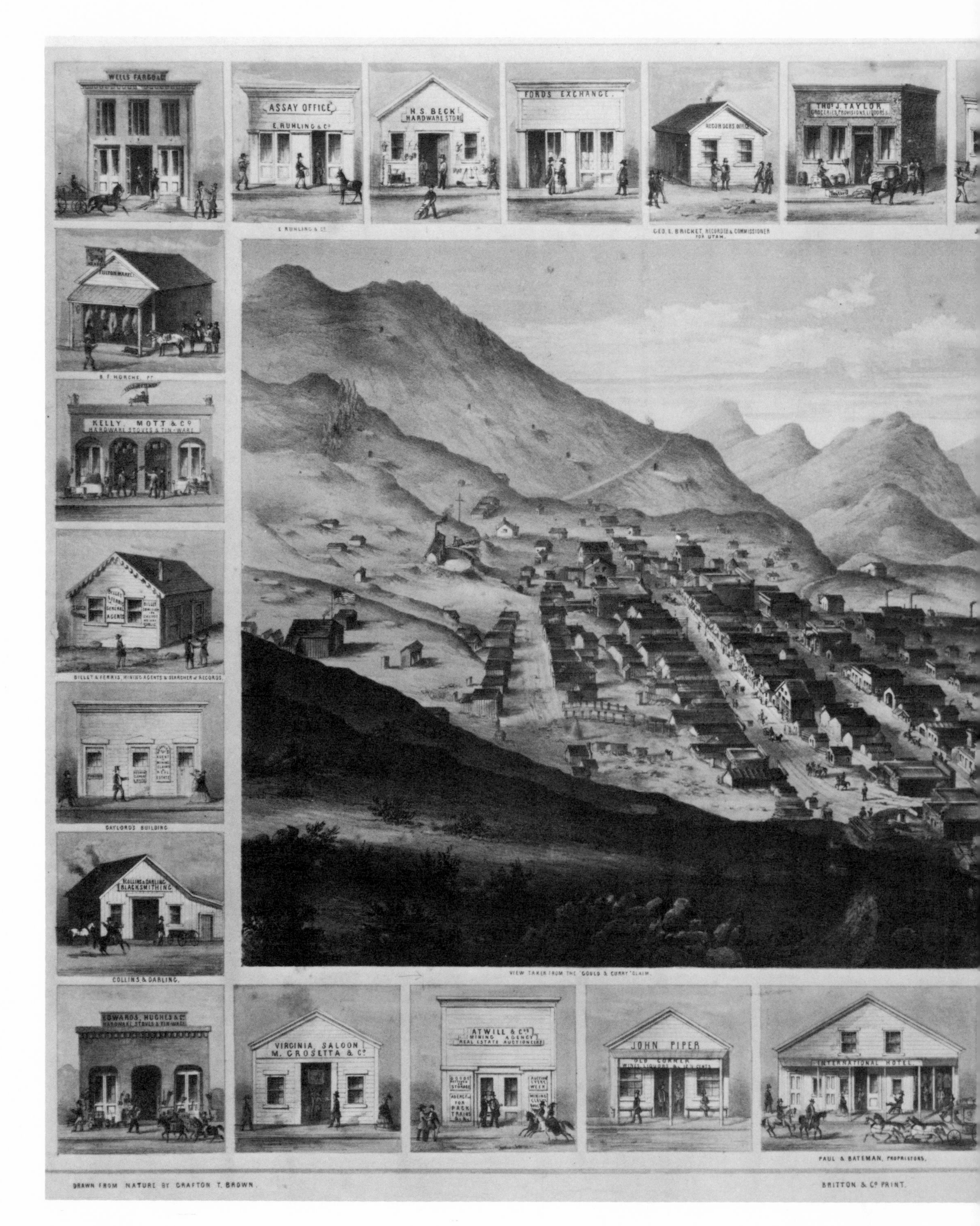
WELLS FARGO & Co
ASSAY OFFICE
E. RUHLING & Co
H.S. BECK
HARDWARE STORE
FORDS EXCHANGE
RECORDERS OFFICE
THOs J. TAYLOR
GROCERIES, PROVISIONS, LIQUORS &c
E. RUHLING & Co
GEO. L. BRICKET, RECORDER & COMMISSIONER FOR UTAH
KELLY, MOTT & Co
HARDWARE STOVES & TIN-WARE
BILLET & FERRIS, MINING AGENTS & SEARCHER of RECORDS
GAYLORDS BUILDING
BLACKSMITHING
COLLINS & DARLING
VIEW TAKEN FROM THE "GOULD & CURRY" CLAIM
EDWARDS, HUGHES & Co
VIRGINIA SALOON
M. GROSETTA & Co
ATWILL & Co
MINING AGENCY
REAL ESTATE AUCTIONEERS
JOHN PIPER
INTERNATIONAL HOTEL
PAUL & BATEMAN, PROPRIETORS
DRAWN FROM NATURE BY GRAFTON T. BROWN
BRITTON & Co PRINT

And, thirdly, it *was* important that any area containing precious metal mines be solidly pro-Union to discourage the South from acquiring any additional monetary support. The Comstock mines were indeed such a factor in the push for Nevada statehood, but they were certainly not the foremost one as the area was teetering on the brink of a major depression.

It was the beginning of this depression which ushered in William Sharon, perhaps the most influential man ever to have a hand in shaping the destiny of Virginia City. Earlier in 1864 Sharon had quit his banking partnership of some years in San Francisco to begin a new venture. With William Ralston and Darius O. Mills he founded the Bank of California, then immediately left for Virginia City to reach his financial tentacles into Nevada. It took little time to organize once he arrived on the Comstock and in November the Virginia City Agency of the Bank of California was opened for business.

Charles De Long, a prominent Comstock attorney, had written a letter in May which stated, "...never since 1860 has Virginia been so dull as during the last few weeks...Stocks are down; money is high, and impossible to obtain even at the higher rates." What few bank loans that were available carried the then-current fee of 5% interest, but Sharon happily began loaning money to mines and mills at a rate of 2%.

The depression continued to deepen, and mines which had recently been productive began levying assessments instead of paying dividends. Still Sharon loaned money, gambling with the elan of a born adventurer. He even allowed extensive overdrafts on many accounts, but as the mines and mills were increasingly unable to pay their debts the bank began to acquire them.

These 1861 views of the Gould & Curry Mining Co. were first published in a promotional book issued to attract investors. One of the buildings shown in the overall view (top) houses the stamp mill (right) where ore was crushed prior to the extraction of gold and silver. In another view, deep below the surface, miners excavate the ore from stopes supported by square set timbering (below).

Lower Gold Hill in 1865, looking west up Crown Point Ravine (left). Photographed the same year, a group of Gold Hill miners pose in front of a mine adit.

The two views below show the heart of Virginia City's business districts in the 1860's. Schools and churches were built alongside pioneer business establishments that flourished before the coming of the railroad.

ERRA VALLEY
LUMBER.
VIRGINIA
PUBLIC

1200 SHARES.

$500 EACH.

25

INTER. REVENUE

GOLD HILL DISTRICT,

No. 28

MATAMORAS

Storey County, N. T.

Gold and Silver Mining

INCORPORAT

Jan. 27, 186

This Certifies That

Ten Shares in the Capital Stock of the

Transferable on the Books of the Company by endorsement hereon and surre

James Scott

Gold Hill News Print.

Secretary.

CAPITAL STOCK-$600.000.

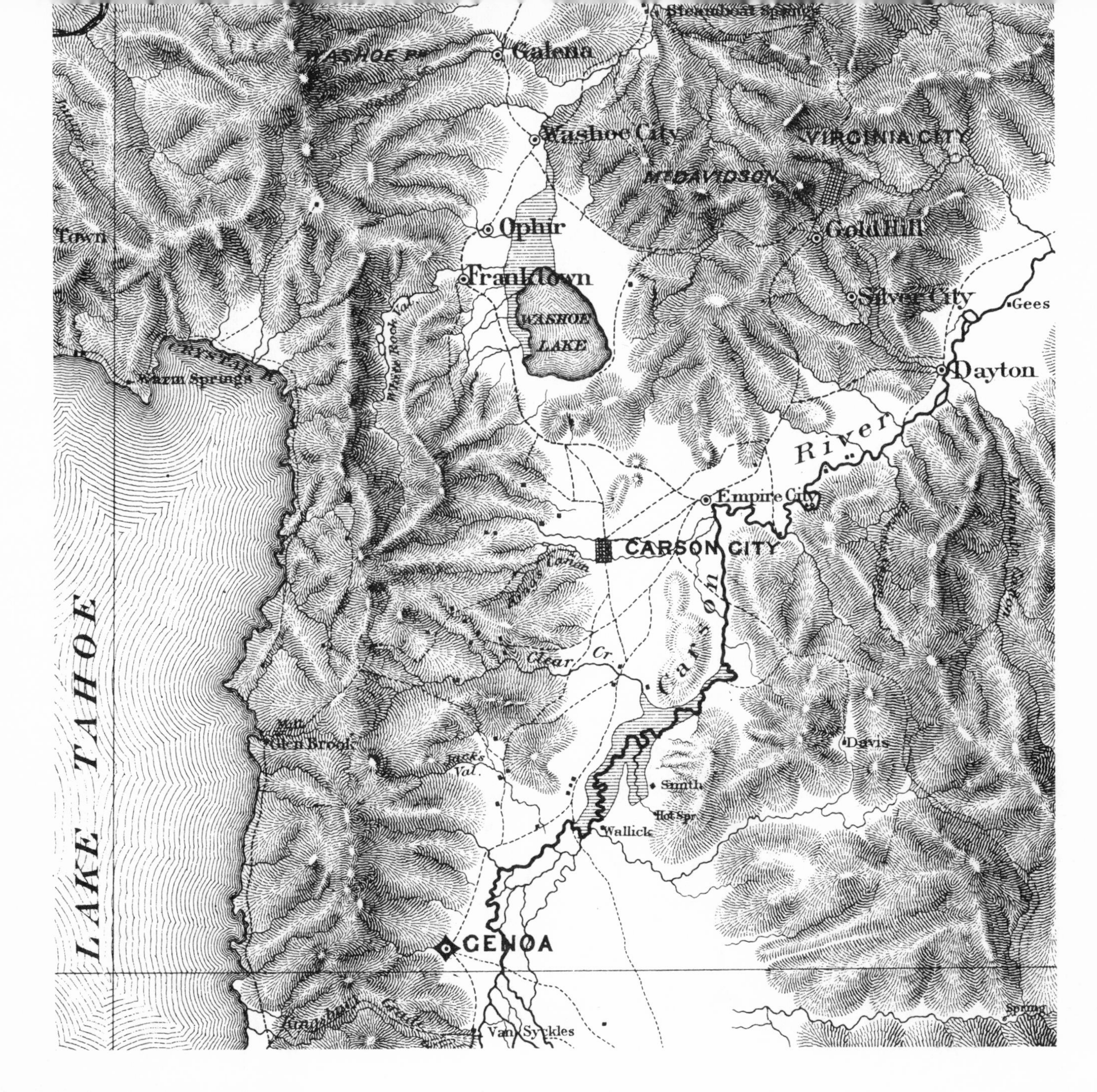

The second International hotel, in existence from 1863 to 1875, was one of the most opulent inns of its day in the Far West (upper left). Area map of western Nevada in the late 1860's shows Virginia City's position in relation to other nearby communities. A typical early stock certificate shows the ornate printing common during the territorial years.

Government agent J. Ross Browne visited the Comstock in 1860 and again three years later. He found the area much livelier on his second visit, as shown by these sketches, since he happened to arrive during the height of the "Rush of '63."

SCENE IN VIRGINIA CITY.

HOME FOR THE BOYS.

HAULING ORE TO THE MILLS.

DIVIDENDS.

AUCTION SALES EVERY DAY.

THE "ROUGHS."

"STAND ASIDE, GENTS."

ASSESSMENTS.

In 1865 the Comstock finally reached the bottom of its first period of borrasca. All of the major mines had played out at depths of 500 feet or less, including the high-grade ore deposit discovered in the Yellow Jacket in 1863 which had produced more than $3.8 million. The catastrophe was enormous — fifty working mines on the Comstock, which had levied millions of dollars of assessments, shut down or reduced to a skeleton work force. At the same time more than 400 wildcat mining companies, whose stocks had been freely traded less than two years earlier, were forced to dissolve.

The true crash occurred in October and its effects were appalling. The total market value of all the Comstock mines, which had been estimated at $40 million in 1863, was only $4 million in mid-December. The value of mining stocks plummeted, wiping out large and small investors alike. Some ten thousand people who suddenly found themselves out of work or penniless were forced to pack up and move on. Some went on to other mining camps while others returned to California, but all carried tales of the Comstock's great panic of 1865.

Not everyone was discouraged though. William Sharon quietly gained control of mine after mine during these perilous times, always believing that the future of the Comstock was desined to be bright. By 1867 he controlled seven mills and numerous mines, including the Yellow Jacket and the Chollar-Potosi. To handle this ever-growing conglomeration, Sharon and three others formed the Union Mill & Mining Company, which within two years had acquired all the major mines and ten additional mills.

The crash was fortunately short-lived. Beginning in 1866 one mine after another hit deposits of paying ore, once more returning prosperity to Virginia City. One such little bonanza was found in the Kentuck mine in Gold Hill, which had been acquired by John Mackay and J. M. Walker during the 1865 depression. It was only a small claim, covering only 94 feet of the Comstock Lode, but on January 1, 1866, a ten-foot vein of ore was found on the 275-foot level. From then until the end of 1869 it produced more than $3.6 million and infuriated Sharon by remaining one of the few good mines to elude his grasp.

The years 1867-68 saw gradual increases in the productivity of the Comstock, but 1869 proved to be eventful in a number of ways. The previous year the partnership of Mackay, Fair, Flood, and O'Brien had begun purchasing stock in the Hale & Norcross mine, one of Sharon's recent acquisitions. By the time of the company's general election in March, 1869, enough stock was in their hands to enable them to wrest control away from the Bank of California. For the second time Sharon was butting heads with the only group powerful and shrewd enough to give him any competition.

Then on April 7 the greatest single disaster ever to befall a Comstock mine occurred. Fire broke out on the 800-foot level of the Yellow Jacket mine, probably caused by an unattended miner's candle, and burned unnoticed for several hours. With the arrival of the morning shift, part of the mine collapsed, and the resulting explosion drove the fire into two adjoining mines — the Crown Point and the Kentuck. The fire was too intense to fight so on April 12, after every attempt to extinguish the blaze had failed, all three mine shafts were sealed and their underground workings were repeatedly pumped full of steam. The dead miners numbered 37, and it took three years before the last smouldering traces of this mine fire were extinguished.

1869 also saw Sharon's greatest bid for true monopoly of the Comstock when he, Mills, and Ralston set about to build the Virginia & Truckee Railroad. By controlling the major mines, the reduction mills along the Carson River, and the means of transportation between the two, Sharon and his "Bank Crowd" would have a virtual stranglehold on the Comstock. The line was completed to Carson City on November 12, then it was extended to Reno to connect with the newly-completed Central Pacific Railroad.

But in the following year Sharon's gamble nearly failed. Production dropped off severely, more and more mines began encountering problems with water in their workings, and many stockholders refused to continue to pay assessments, sending prices of individual shares down to rock bottom. Minor ore bodies were discovered in the Yellow Jacket and Chollar-Potosi, but shares of the Crown Point fell to $2, the Consolidated Virginia was going begging at $1 a share, and water up to the 800-foot level plummeted Belcher stock to $1 also.

The stability and confidence which had been so slowly regained after the panic of 1865 were again destroyed. During 1870 residents once more moved away, many to the then-booming camps of Pioche and Eureka, while Sharon and his "Bank Crowd" were on the edge of financial disaster. The Bank of California was reported to have $3 million invested in the Comstock at that time, three-fifths of the bank's total capital, yet the market value of the Comstock mines had fallen below its previous low record of $4 million. Adolph Sutro, who had just begun digging his ambitious four-mile drainage tunnel, was about to close down. The entire future of the Comstock Lode was in danger.

Then just at the close of the year a discovery in the Crown Point mine, which had been so badly damaged

From his office in the Bank of California building on South C Street in Virginia City, William Sharon acquired and orchestrated his enormous holdings of Comstock industry.

in the Yellow jacket fire of a little over a year earlier, changed the entire picture. The ore body was developed quietly and without fanfare, but Alvinza Hayward, one of Sharon's associates, immediately began buying stock. By the time Sharon realized what was happening Hayward had gained control of the mine. Its stock jumped from $3 a share to $300, then when the same ore body was found to extend into the Belcher ground, which Sharon also controlled, that stock also skyrocketed from $7.50 to $240 per share. Another small but rich ore deposit was found in the Chollar-Potosi mine, and the Comstock was again on the road to recovery.

Though a small stock market crash occurred early in May, aided in good part by Sharon, the Crown Point and the Belcher immediately stabilized. They continued to be among the very few Nevada mines to pay dividends. Sharon ran unsuccessfully for a U.S. Senator's seat in 1872, then once again settled down to the management of his enormous empire. But the activity of another mine was on the horizon, and its success would wreak havoc with Sharon's plans.

The Consolidated Virginia mine, in Virginia City proper, was created in 1867 by the merger of the Sides, the White & Murphy, and the original California mines. Difficulties quickly arose and the main shaft was not begun until 1869. Then as the workings were driven deeper the ore began to pinch out. By mid-1870, when work was finally suspended, stockholders had paid more than $1 million into the property without finding any worthwhile ore.

But though the Con. Virginia had not produced any profit at all, John Mackay believed it to be "a good gamble." He and his partners, Fair, Floor, and O'Brien, quietly purchased Con. Virginia stock at less than $12 a share until they owned about three-fourths of the total shares. In January, 1872, the new owners took control and immediately planned various ways of continuing the development of the mine. Numerous proposals for extending the main shaft or digging horizontal drifts at various levels were all luckily abandoned when William Sharon gave his permission to let them use his Gould & Curry shaft to begin a new exploration. He is reported to have gleefully remarked, "I'll help those Irishmen lose some of their Hale & Norcross money," but that was not to be.

The new drift had been driven in 978 feet, and was well into Con. Virginia ground, when a low-grade vein was found on September 12, 1872. The decision was made to follow the vein, even though it led away from the main Comstock Lode, but as the ore was low-grade work progressed "conservatively." Then on March 1, 1873, the *Gold Hill News* made the first announcement of a major strike in the Con. Virginia.

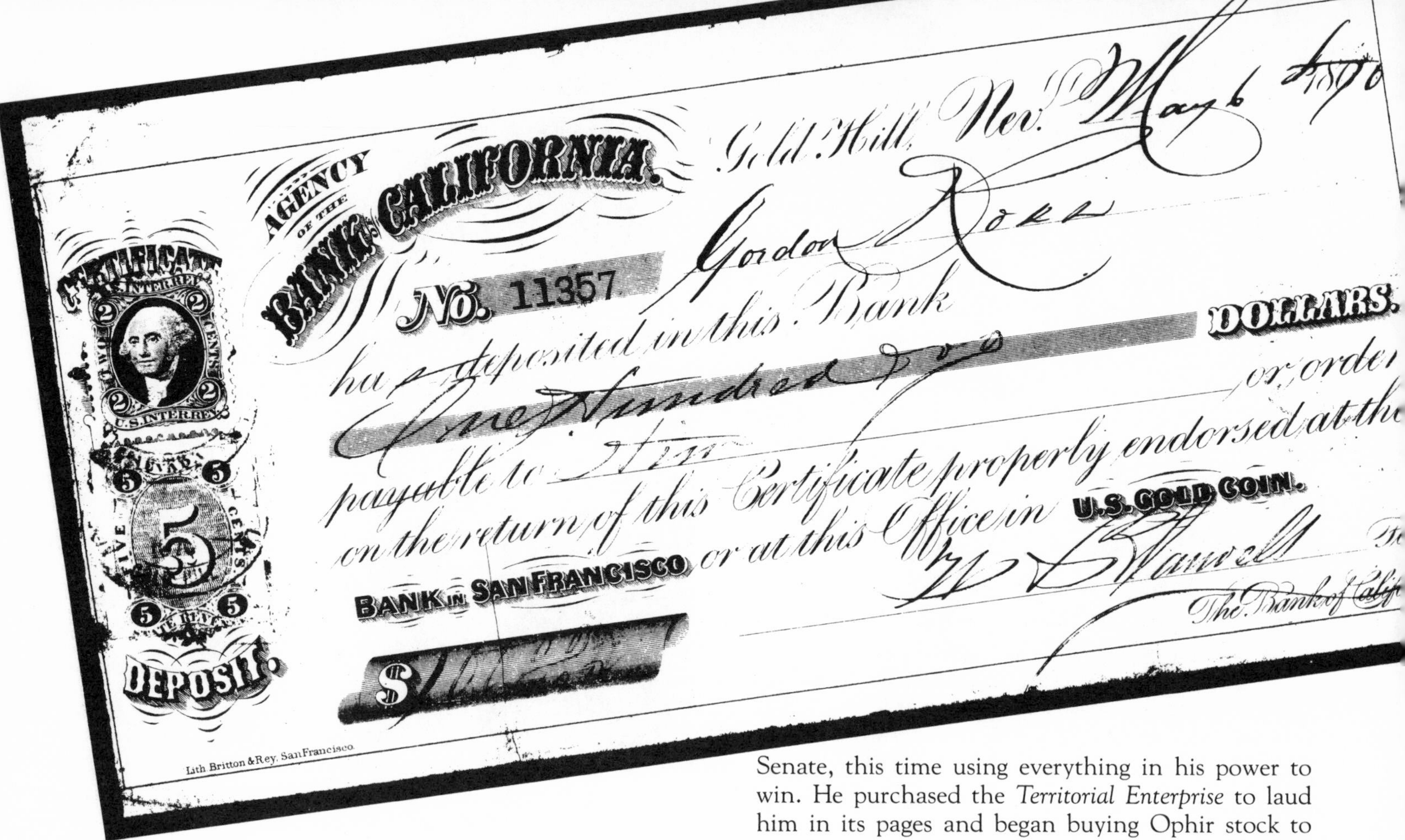

CERTIFICATE OF DEPOSIT.

AGENCY OF THE BANK OF CALIFORNIA. Gold Hill, Nev. May 6

No. 11357 Gordon Ross

has deposited in this Bank One Hundred DOLLARS.

payable to or order

on the return of this Certificate properly endorsed at the BANK IN SAN FRANCISCO, or at this Office in U.S. GOLD COIN.

The Bank of Calif

$100

Lith Britton & Rey. San Francisco.

This was no small pocket of high-grade, as had been found in other Comstock mines, but it was the granddaddy of all Nevada orebodies. Located 1,200 feet directly below the streets of Virginia City, the discovery soon came to be called the "Big Bonanza" and its discovery sent shockwaves through mining and financial circles. Mackay and his associates, soon known as the "Bonanza Firm," put all their respective weight and resources into developing a producing mining operation. Believing the orebody to pitch to the south they bought control of the adjoining Best & Belcher mine, then acquired the Gould & Curry just south of that. To the north they bought the Kinney, Central, and Central No. 2 mines, and with the ground of the old California mine, incorporated these properties into a new company called the California. A joint shaft, known as the C&C and serving both the Con. Virginia and the California mines, was begun 1,000 feet east of the Con. Virginia shaft and was eventually used as the main access to the Big Bonanza.

In 1874 Mackay and his associates built the Con. Virginia mill and the California pan mill. These businesses were completely separate from the mines, allowing the Bonanza Firm to pay themselves the going rate for milling their own ore. Then all of these businesses were incorporated together under the name of the Pacific Mill & Mining Company.

Sharon did not feel he was through on the Comstock though. In 1874 he again decided to run for the Senate, this time using everything in his power to win. He purchased the *Territorial Enterprise* to laud him in its pages and began buying Ophir stock to attempt to wrest its control away from E. J. "Lucky" Baldwin. In the ensuing stock manipulations all Comstock shares were again drawn upward — California stock reaching $780, Con. Virginia peaking at $710, and Ophir stock climbing from $20 to $315 even after Sharon had gained control and been elected to the Senate. On January 7, 1875, the market value of the Comstock mines was estimated at $300 million, as compared with only $4 million in 1860.

Then on January 8 the financial bubble once again burst. Canny stock manipulators took their profits and ran, leaving thousands of investors broken and bankrupt. For six weeks the market fell, with ten leading mines losing a paper value of more than $17 million in just one day. Shares in the Con. Virginia dropped to $450, while California mine stock fell to $250, and the Ophir bottomed at $65 after its all-time high of $315.

But even if Comstock shares had been inflated, the Big Bonanza was very real, and the market stabilized in mid-February. Soon business in Virginia City was back to normal, with the population growing faster than houses could be built. Once more the future seemed destined to be bright, though on a lesser get-rich-quick level than before the last stock crash.

While things were on the upswing in Virginia City, the Bank of California was in serious trouble. William Ralston had been rapidly shuffling assets out of sheer desperation to try to keep the bank from failing, but on August 26, 1875, operations were suspended in the middle of the afternoon. Soon afterwards Ralston put all his affairs in order, made a new will, and went swimming in San Francisco Bay. His body washed ashore later that day, but it is still unknown if death was by suicide or accident.

It took a number of days to reorganize but with the help of such millionaires as Mills, Sharon, and "Lucky" Baldwin more than $7 million was raised to recapitalize the bank. It reopened on October 2, and as an indication of how much it affected the Comstock Lode, two mining exchanges had immediately ceased operations when the bank closed and did not reopen until October 5.

Mackay and the Bonanza Firm had long been planning to open a bank of their own to compete with the Bank of California, but their plans had no bearing on the near-failure of Sharon's bank. Once all was in readiness though, they formed the Nevada Bank of San Francisco with a capital of $5 million in gold. On October 4 they opened for business, and a branch was located on C Street in Virginia City, directly across from the Bank of California.

Then on October 26, 1875, disaster again struck Virginia City when a woman called "Crazy Kate" went out to the barn to milk a cow at 6 a.m. The cow kicked over a lantern which ignited loose hay in the barn, and the fire was a runaway before anyone had time to report it.

There had been no rain for months and a strong wind was blowing. Soon block after block was aflame with thousands of people scrambling to save what they could before the fire reached them. Among the losses was all the fire-fighting equipment in Virginia City except for just a few pieces owned by volunteer fire companies. Only dynamite could stop the fire so crews systematically set about clearing firebreaks.

Down at the mines every effort was made to keep the fire out of the workings. If it had swept underground the Comstock would have been wiped out, due to the miles of interconnected stopes and drifts and the millions of feet of timber used in their support. Mackay was hard at work at the Con. Virginia shaft sealing the collar with dirt when a woman came up to beg for assistance in saving the Catholic church. He reportedly answered, "Damn the church! We can build another if we can keep the fire from going down these shafts." The surface buildings of the Con Virginia were destroyed but the mine itself was saved, and Mackay was the largest contributor to the reconstruction of the church.

The Ophir mine attempted the same method of sealing their shaft but was not as successful. Fire destroyed their headframe and also burned some 400 feet down the shaft, but it was extinguished before any of the main workings could be destroyed. The only other mine casualties were the Con. Virginia mill and the California crushing plant, but a half-mile square section directly in the heart of the city was totally ruined.

The map's dark portion shows the area destroyed in the great fire of 1875.

By noon the fire was under control, having caused an estimated $10 million in damages. More than 2,000 people were homeless and the weather was turning cold, so a call went out for assistance. Communities around the West responded, with the V&T RR sending 46 trains over the single-line track to Virginia City in one day. From Reno, Carson City, and as far away as San Francisco came loads of medicine, food, blankets, and clothes. The dispossessed were cared for first, then came re-construction.

The value of Virginia City mining stocks had crashed with the first reports of the fire, but the determination to rebuild the city bigger and better than ever was strong. St. Mary's Catholic church was replaced by one of the most beautiful 19th century churches in Nevada. The International hotel was rebuilt into a magnificent brick structure six stories high, of the most opulent furnishings, and containing 160 rooms. All up and down B and C Streets saloons, stores, fraternal halls, and hotels were quickly replaced, often with brick, and many of these buildings are still standing today.

Almost immediately after the terrible fire of 1875, Virginia City started to rebuild. It soon became the principal city between Denver and San Francisco, thanks to the fever of speculation and production sparked by the recent discovery of the "Big Bonanza." This scene, taken from Cedar Hill north of town, shows Geiger Grade in the extreme foregound where it enters Virginia City and becomes C Street. Substantial brick and stone buildings mark the center of town, where the major businesses influenced activity not only throughout the rest of Nevada but in other parts of the West as well. Traveling photographer J. H. Crockwell took this shot in 1885 and it has since become a classic, illustrating this prominent silver mining city at a point very near the peak of its glory years.

CENTENNIAL
M. E. Church
A.D. 1876

ER BRO'S
rters of
INE
THING
TELEGRAPH

After the 1875 fire numerous ornate and well-constructed buildings arose in Virginia City. Piper's Opera House, on B Street, was designed to host the finest of the theatrical performances then available (upper left). The distinctive lines of the Methodist church made it an attractive structure, though overshadowed by the grandeur of St. Mary's Catholic church in the background. South C Street, showing the Bank of California building with the International hotel in the background, was crowded with the throngs of people who came to the Comstock during the "Big Bonanza" years (bottom, facing page). This unusual view (above) of the rear B Street entrance of the third and largest International hotel shows its location directly across the street from Piper's Opera House.

The Ophir mine shipped all of its ore by rail once the V&T RR extended a siding in the early 1870's which ran alongside its ore chutes (above). Inside the Ophir's main hoisting works three miners pose in front of the double-stacked cages in the massive 3-compartment shaft (left). An early view of Gold Hill's major mines (upper right) shows some of the names made prominent during the 1860's and 1870's, though few became as well-known as the major Virginia City mines. A view of Gold Hill looking north illustrates how large this community had grown by the late 1870's (right).

EMPIRE
IMPERIAL

The discovery of the "Big Bonanza" in the Consolidated Virginia mine (lower left) produced a boom era unequalled in silver mining history. By the late 1870's the "Bonanza Era" had witnessed the peak growth of Virginia City (upper left), making it a true metropolis on the barren flanks of Sun Mountain.

1876 proved to be a banner year for Virginia City. Population reached its all-time peak of nearly 23,000 persons, meaning that about 49% of all Nevadans lived on the Comstock. The Big Bonanza really began to pay off as both the Con. Virginia and the California, two of the three Comstock mines which were then paying dividends instead of levying assessments, were each returning more than $1 million monthly to their stockholders. Together these two mines produced $30,058,490 in 1876 alone.

This huge outpouring of money was not limited to the stockholders either. Miners were making the then-high wage of $4 per shift and most mines were operating day and night. Because of the constant stream of men entering and leaving the mines, many Comstock businesses seldom closed. Saloons in Virginia City dispensed such quantities of one-bit (12½¢) drinks that liquor revenue was near $1 million for the year. In 1880, four years after the height of the boom, some 75,000 gallons of liquor and 225,000 gallons of beer were consumed on the Comstock, and it was considered a "dry" year compared with 1876.

Prices for other goods were relatively high though. Chickens cost $10 a dozen, sugar was up to 18¢ per pound, dried apples were 20¢ a pound, beef cost 25¢ a pound, and coffee ran 40¢ a pound. Rent cost around $16 a month for a single room, room and board together in a boardinghouse ran up to $45 per month, and the average charge for a restaurant meal was 50 to 75 cents.

At the peak of its glory Virginia City was a booming, roisterous, 24-hour a day town, boasting live theatre productions ranging from Shakespeare to Mazeppa, many newspapers including two dailies, a number of fraternal and social organizations, and an infrastructure of other recreational facilities ranging from the dignified card and billiard rooms of the Washoe Club to the opium dens of Chinatown. Money flowed with abandon, enabling even the average miner to occasionally sample the traditional Comstock treat of fresh oysters and champagne.

But spectacular though it was, the boom was short-lived. The great orebody that was the Big Bonanza petered out on the 1650-foot level, sending the value of the stock of the two great mines into rapid decline. A strong bear attack on the market early in 1876 had considerably lowered share prices already but they fell to absurd levels in the fall of 1877 when Con. Virginia was quoted at $21.25 and California stock was bringing $23.50.

The Bonanza Firm, refusing to believe that the glory days were coming to a close, bought control of mine after mine in the hope of striking another massive silver deposit. In rapid succession they acquired the Yellow Jacket, Ophir, Mexican, Union, and

CIGARS
BULL RUN ALLEY
CHOP AND SAUSAGE HOUSE
"WASHEE, WASHEE"
A STREET COBBLER

A NEVADA SILVER MINE—CHANGING THE SHIFT.—

CHINESE QUARTERS, VIRGINIA CITY, NEVADA.

Sierra Nevada mines, then spent millions searching vainly for another Big Bonanza.

O'Brien died in 1878, and Fair resigned all active participation the same year to run for the U.S. Senate against Sharon whose term expired in 1880. The Bank of California's power had been so eclipsed since the discovery of the Big Bonanza that Fair was able to buy his Senate seat with ease, although after being elected he proved to be a "do-nothing" more interested in his title than in accomplishing anything.

As production dropped off, the mines naturally began to reduce their work force. By the end of 1877 more than 2,000 men were unemployed with the number growing daily. A minor high-grade deposit called the Hardy vein was found in the Ophir mine, causing renewed optimism that fortunes were again on the rise. But by mid-1878, with unemployment again creeping upward, men once more began to desert the Comstock.

Up to a thousand men left that fall, most to the reactivated California mining town of Bodie. That same year the *San Francisco Chronicle* began a vitriolic campaign against the Bonanza Firm, culminating in a court decision awarding damages to stockholders. Only one nail was left to seal the coffin tight on the last of the Comstock's Big Bonanza boom, and this was driven home with the "Sierra Nevada deal."

Located on the extreme northern end of the Comstock Lode, the Sierra Nevada mine had never made more than a moderate showing in all its years of operation. Suddenly in mid-1878 its stock began climbing steadily and unaccountably, while its owner hinted at a new orebody to be unveiled when he had acquired enough additional stock. A fever of speculation dragged other Comstock stocks upward as well, until even Fair and Flood began speculating heavily in Sierra Nevada stock and that of the Union, another North End mine. Mining men and newspaper reporters alike shouted optimism when allowed to view the underground workings and another bonanza seemed eminent. Then on September 27 the market peaked, with Sierra Nevada stock at $280 and Union at $182. A slight decline followed until three weeks later when the market suddenly panicked. Sierra Nevada shares crashed to $65 within two days, wreaking the worst financial destruction ever witnessed among Comstock investors.

The Comstock began a steady decline with population slowly but inexorably starting to dwindle, but the vibrant lifestyle managed to continue. In 1879 ex-President U.S. Grant visited Virginia City for three days and the town "put on the dog" as it had never done before. Not to be outdone, President Hayes and Major General Sherman visited the following year,

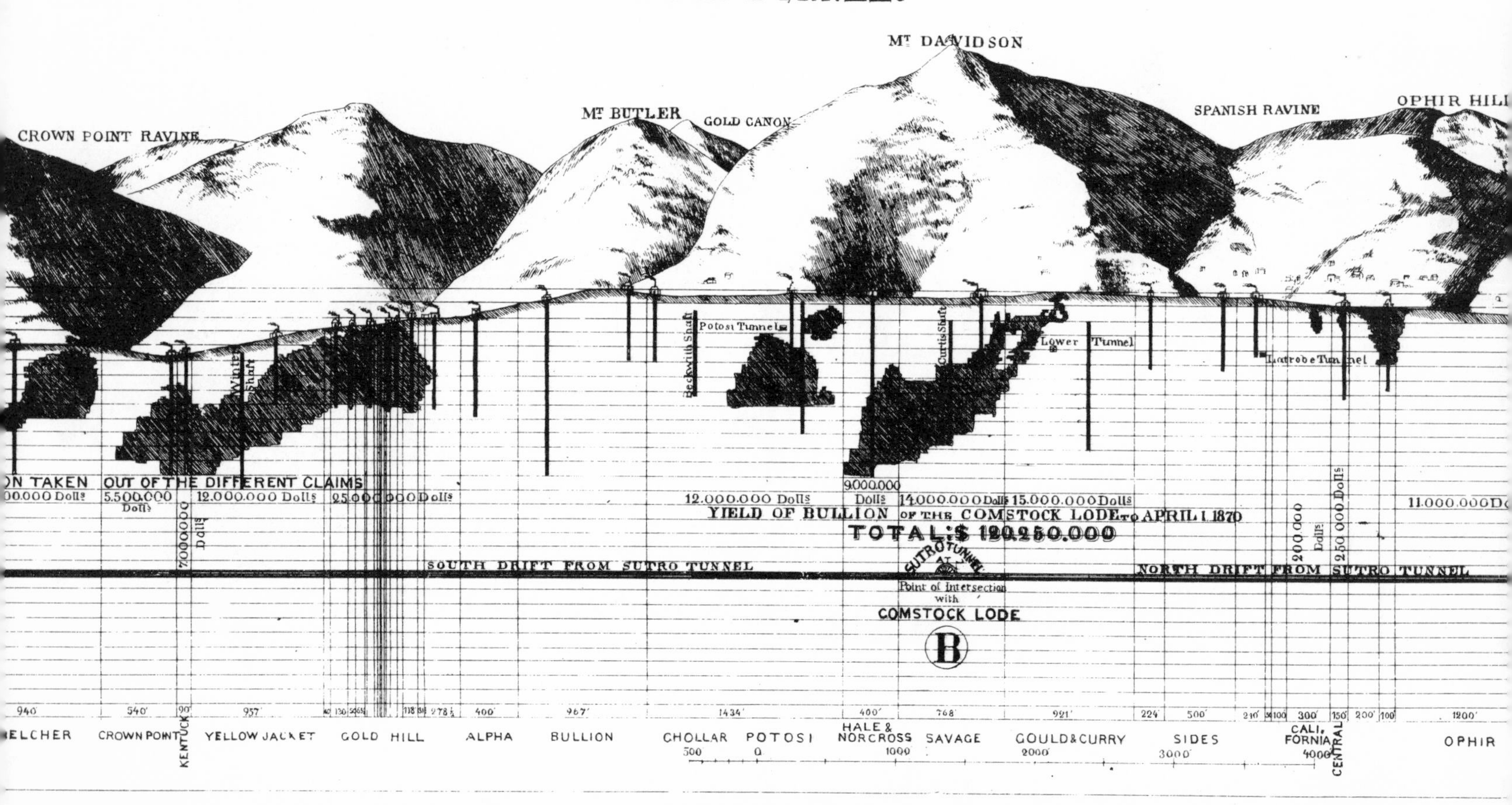

Winter entertainment in Virginia often included sleigh rides on the snow-covered streets.

but their fete was not as spectacular as they stayed but one day.

By 1880 everyone knew that the "Bonanza Era" was over. The Con. Virginia paid its last dividend, the California had ceased paying them the previous year, and stock transactions slowed to a trickle on the California markets. But as bonanzas go, it had been a humdinger. From 1874 to 1880 the California and the Con. Virginia had produced $105,014,498 of which $74,250,000 had been paid on dividends. All told, Comstock mines had produced about $320 million in the 21 years between 1859 and 1880.

Where the Big Bonanza orebody had been removed a giant timber-filled cavern was left, supported by 150 million board feet of square set timbering. In 1881 fire broke out in this stope and all entrances to it were sealed. Slowly the ground over the stope settled, a long crack appeared in the mountainside above town, and even portions of Virginia City itself slid a slight distance downhill. Deep mining was attempted

Gold Hill looking south from the Divide, c. 1880's.

These photos illustrate daily life on the Comstock during its heyday. A blacksmith pauses at his anvil; a hay wagon delivers feed grown in the lower valleys to a Virginia City stable; and the members of the Virginia City Camera Club pose with their equipment in front of a local attorney's office.

NEVADA
LIVERY & FEED STABLE.
BOARDING & TRANSIENT STABLE

below the area of the stope, but it proved a failure and in 1884 the lower workings were abandoned and allowed to fill with water. At this time Con. Virginia stock fell to the previously-unbelievable price of 5¢ per share.

In 1883, Senator John Jones acquired a lease on the Con. Virginia, believing that the removal of low-grade ore would prove profitable. One stipulation of the lease was that the fire still smouldering in the Big Bonanza stope had to be extinguished, which Jones accomplished by pumping it full of carbonic acid gas. By 1885 he was ready to begin operations and within six months had recovered more than $310,000 from low-grade ore above the 1550-foot level. His success prompted the reorganization of the two great mines into the Consolidated California & Virginia Mining Co., which now wanted to take over the profitable venture themselves. They offered him a third interest in a new milling company if he would surrender his lease, which he did on the first day of 1886.

The Con. Cal. & Virginia entered into a 10-year period of profitable low-grade mining, beginning with the discovery of a nice little orebody on the 1400-foot level of the California mine. It was this discovery which brought about "The 1886 Deal." When the stock manipulations were over the Con. Cal. & Virginia was still very much alive and was proving that shallow mining of low-grade ore could be done at a profit.

As no major orebodies had been recently found below the 1600-foot level in any Comstock mine, and as the expenses and difficulty of deep mining increased enormously as the shafts were sunk below the 3000-foot level, it was finally decided to abandon the deep workings.

The Combination mine was the last to cease pumping, shutting theirs down on October 16, 1886. Immediately its lower levels were flooded, as were those of the Chollar, Potosi, Hale & Norcross, and Savage mines.

Deep mining was over, but by 1888 the Con. Cal. & Virginia had located additional low-grade ore in the rock used to backfill the stopes mined in 1876-77. There had been such a rush during the height of the Big Bonanza to locate additional high-grade deposits that much of the lesser rock had been overlooked. More than $1 million was paid in dividends on Con. Cal. & Virginia stock in 1888, just from the mining of this lesser-quality ore.

The last small orebody was found in 1895, when a very small deposit was located on the 1650-foot level of the California. It enabled the mine to pay more than $200,000 in dividends that year, but the days of large Comstock productions were over. John Mackay finally saw that the end was at hand, selling out all his interests on the Comstock to some California

This view shows a Reno military band parading south on B Street early in the 20th century, with the International hotel looming in the background.

stock brokers. He was not alone, as more and more mine owners, investors, businessmen, and residents were departing the Comstock for more lucrative areas.

The total production of the 29 mines still in operation in 1898 was only $205,000 and their stocks were practically worthless. As usual, it was the brokers who dreamed up one last scheme to glean a bit more revenue from the Comstock. The plan was to pump out the mines from the Con. Virginia to the Sierra Nevada, on the north end of the lode, to resume deep mining once again. The Comstock Pumping Association was formed to do the actual work, pumping water from the interconnected workings through the old C&C shaft.

The whole idea was to once again inflate Virginia City mining stocks so that the brokers could make a last killing. However, the plan backfired when one small orebody of high-grade after another was located below the 1800-foot level. In the first two decades of this century some $7 million was recovered from the four mines affected, but extremely high pumping expenses reduced the actual profit to about $500,000.

In 1903 an attempt was made to unwater the "middle mines," namely the Gould & Curry through the Chollar-Potosi, by pumping through the Ward shaft. However, water temperatures up to 175 degrees and an extremely high volume of water soon proved too much to handle.

Things were stagnant, compared to the Big Bonanza yeas, but attempts were still made to work the last of the low-grade ore. For a 15-year period beginning in 1908 the Chollar-Potosi was worked this way, prompting the construction of a new mill in Six-Mile Canyon. During the same period the Yellow Jacket, Crown Point, and Belcher mines in Gold Hill joined forces to build a new cyanide mill. This new milling process gave returns of up to 93% of the gold and 86% of the silver in Comstock ores.

Practical recovery of low-grade ore encouraged New York capitalists to finance the United Comstock Mines Company in 1920. A 2,000-ton-a-day cyanide plant was built in American Flat while a 9,250-foot tunnel was driven up to the Gold Hill mines to deliver ore and tailings by gravity. This project was one of the most modern in the world for its time, but after only two years of operation it was sold at a loss. Even though $3 million had been recovered, milling costs were almost the same as the amount produced. The new owners, Comstock Merger Mines, operated the mill until 1927, when the operation was abandoned and the equipment dismantled.

After a five-year lull during the peak of the Depression, the U.S. Government raised the value of gold

Pogonip, a local Indian name for an ice fog, hovers close to the ground near the Fourth Ward School (left). C Street looking north near the turn of the century shows a local bakery delivery wagon. A plethora of plucked poultry is featured at Virginia City's Hatch Brothers market.

C Street in the winter is often lined with heaps of snow while during the summer brisk winds frequently swirl down its entire length.

to $35 per ounce and silver to 64¢. Almost immediately new mining operations were begun, but by this time a technique new to the Comstock was introduced — open-pit mining. The Sierra Nevada open-pitted Cedar Hill just north of Virginia City, while the Con. Virginia began excavating the surface of the original Ophir mine as well as on their own property. The Arizona Comstock Company took over a half mile of the lode, encompassing the Chollar through the Hale & Norcross mines to begin open-pitting the Loring Cut across the street from the Fourth Ward School. The tracks of the V&T RR were rerouted to allow the Sutro Tunnel Coalition to excavate the Crown Point mine, while they also operated an open-pit mine on the Imperial ground just below Greiner's Bend in Gold Hill. A seventh pit, located on the Overman mine in Gold Hill, was also begun by the Consolidated Chollar, Gould, & Savage Mining Co.

All of these operations were worked profitably until World War II broke out. On October 8, 1942, the War Production Board issued an order which severely curtailed the mining of gold and silver. Where production had been in excess of $1.8 million in Storey County in 1941, it was only $24,000 in 1945. By 1950 all mining had ceased and Virginia City's population had declined to its all-time low. Buildings were quickly falling to ruin, antiques and equipment were being hauled away by the truckload to other towns and museums, and the few remaining businesses were barely managing to eke out a meager existence. Fire had destroyed such landmarks as the International Hotel, the Frederick's building, and the Marye building, leaving vacant lots along once-crowded C Street.

Surprisingly, Virginia City did not dry up and blow away, as did almost every other 19th century Nevada mining town. Instead the Comstock saw the arrival of Lucius Beebe and Charles Clegg, a pair of East Coast *bon vivants* who were searching to capture a remnant of the flamboyance and notoriety of the Old West's glory years. Virginia City fit the bill and, since they could bring their private railroad car no closer than Carson City, they purchased and restored a mansion on A Street.

Their main contribution, though, was the reactivation of the then-defunct *Territorial Enterprise*. With several best-selling non-fiction books already under their belts, this pioneer newspaper provided an outlet for their more humorous, irreverent, and often exaggerated pieces. Their special style of writing, coupled with their many prominent contacts in major cities throughout the U.S., also attracted major advertisers and boosted circulation. This, more than any other single cause, prompted the present-day tourist boom which has kept Virginia City alive and kicking for the past three decades.

Museums were opened, old mansions were refurbished for tours, the number of saloons increased dramatically, Piper's Opera House began to host occasional functions, and a number of special attractions such as camel races, quick-draw contests, motorcycle races, and endurance rides were introduced. The sound of a lone visitor's bootheels thumping on the wooden boardwalks increased to a thunder as the number of tourists coming to the Comstock jumped to more than a million annually.

For a time the only silver on the Comstock was that being spent by tourists. But as silver coins began to disappear from circulation, following removal of federal price controls, mining men once again started investigating the feasibility of working the area. In 1976 Houston Oil & Minerals acquired much of the Gold Hill portion of the lode, constructed a modern cyanide mill in American Flat, and reopened the Imperial pit just below Greiner's Bend. Soon thereafter underground operations were reactivated in the Savage mine, and the Comstock Lode was gain a productive mining area.

A storm of controversy assailed the Houston operation when its pit attained a size that would soon force the removal of many historic buildings and the relocation of the Gold Hill highway. But before any action could be decided upon, a drastic decline in the price of gold and silver led to a shutdown of the mining operation. In late 1981 the Savage mine also laid off its employees as silver fell below $10 an ounce, and mining on the lode again came to a halt.

Today Beebe and Clegg are gone, the *Territorial Enterprise* has again suspended publication, and the famous mines whose names were once a byword all across the nation are silent and empty. But Virginia City is a unique sort of a town, whose inhabitants have consistently refused to forego its 19th century lifestyle. Business deals are still concluded over a shot of whiskey in its century-old saloons, the fire department is still volunteer, leather-vested Stetson-clad deputies keep it peaceful, and honky-tonk pianos still sound down the street on summer evenings.

From bonanza to borrasca, boom to depression, Virginia City has seen it all more than once. Yet it remains one of the last vestiges of the Old West, and it will always be the First Lady of western mining towns.

Virginia City Today

In some ways Virginia City today has changed very little from what it was in the 19th century. The population, of course, has shrunk from its late-1870's peak of more than 20,000 to a present level of about 700 persons. Mining has once again ceased as well, but a strong tourist economy continues to provide a healthy business atmosphere. In fact, with 22 saloons and bars in operation in Virginia City, the current ratio of one drinking establishment for about every 32 men, women, and children seems outrageously high, until the million or so tourists who visit the Comstock every year are considered.

Services are relatively limited, as is typical for a community of this size. A dedicated and highly-trained volunteer fire department is a source of pride to this previously-devastated, primarily frame-structured town, and they provide emergency medical service as well. Virginia City is still the county seat of Storey County, with the 1876 stone courthouse containing all county offices, a fully-staffed Sheriff's office, and the county jail. As it is an unincorporated community the county has jurisdiction over Virginia City, as well as Gold Hill and the areas known as Mark Twain, at the mouth of Six Mile Canyon; Lockwood, on the Truckee River at the north end of the county; and the new residential development of Virginia Highlands located east of Five Mile Flat on Geiger Grade.

While such amenities as drug stores, supermarkets, hardware stores, or department stores are not available within the county, Virginia City does have a market, a gas station, and a bank is under construction. However, all needed shopping facilities are found only 14 miles away in Carson City or 25 miles to the north in Reno, both of which are readily accessible except during the worst winter storms.

Surprisingly, both summer and winter are relatively mild in Virginia City. Situated at an elevation of 6,220 feet, the monthly temperatures range from a mean of 33 degrees in January to 70 degrees in July. However January, 1956, saw the mercury dip to -3 degrees, while as recently as August, 1970, a high of 100 degrees was recorded. Annual precipitation runs about 12 inches per year, although 9.78 inches occurred in January, 1969, alone. Most of this precipitation falls as winter snow, with 56 inches per year being the mean. The greatest recorded snowfall occurred during the winter of 1889-1890, when 72.5 inches fell just in the month of January. Yet even with the high elevation and sometimes snowy winters, Virginia City's growing season averages 107 days annually. The mean humidity is also mild, averaging 70 percent in winter and 30 percent during the summer.

The community's location on the steep eastern slope of Sun Mountain does occasion a number of very windy days. Known as "Washoe zephyrs," these winds can reach speeds of near 70 miles per hour and have been known to destroy signs, blow chimneys over, and even demolish derelict structures. While they seldom reach that velocity, a slight wind is almost always blowing in town both in winter and summer.

With the main tourist season now extending from May through October, many of the residents are employed in tourist-related businesses. The Comstock's close proximity to both Carson City and Reno has also spurred construction of a number of new homes, with some of the residents commuting to jobs outside the county. New business buildings along C Street have also been constructed recently, while many of the original structures have been updated and refurbished.

Even with these few concessions to the 20th century, Virginia City is still very much a living legend. Most of the sidewalks are wood, horsemen and horse-drawn vehicles clop occasionally up the street, the roar of .45 calibre revolvers still echo during the fast draw contests, and the saloons are still the meeting spots and informal offices of the residents. Historians may have officially stated that the "frontier" no longer existed in the 1890's, and the "Old West" might have passed into oblivion about the time Zane Grey was first becoming popular, but Virginia City consistently refuses to accept these facts, and it may well do so for some time to come.

For More Information...

The heyday of Virginia City and the Comstock Lode has been the subject of many novels, magazine articles, technical mining accounts and general histories. *Nevada An Annotated Bibliography* by Stanley W. Paher lists more than 100 such works, all annotated. That volume should be the beginning point for any serious research of the Comstock era.

Many books on Virginia City are still available, either in original editions or reprint form. Myron F. Angel, [Thompson & West] *History of Nevada 1881,* is a big 680 page volume which is the most used and quoted history of any issued about Nevada and Virginia City.

Hubert H. Bancroft, *History of Nevada...* [1888], has large chapters which discuss the Comstock's mining and political development. This history is strongly entrenched as a source of historical authority.

Francis C. Lincoln, *Mining Districts and Mineral Resources of Nevada*, gives a historical summary, corporate information, and record of production. The Comstock Lode bibliography (pages 229-233) leads the researcher to scores of primary sources.

Eliot Lord, *Comstock Mining and Miners,* is a volume basic to mining and milling on the Comstock to the year of publication, 1883. It is a comprehensive, well written narrative history.

David F. Myrick, *Railroads of Nevada and Eastern California, Volume One*, contains more than a history of the Virginia & Truckee and other railroads. This thoughtful researcher includes politics, economics, and social incidents with illustrations in the chapter which discusses the Comstock Lode (pages 136-162).

Stanley W. Paher, *Nevada Ghost Towns & Mining Camps*, has a fast-paced summary of Virginia City, along with numerous unpublished photographs. There is much discussion of satellite Comstock towns and about 670 other Nevada Ghost Towns. S. W. Paher, editor, *Nevada Towns & Tales, Vol. 1*, has one chapter (pages 85-99) filled with Comstock lore and short stories, along with illustrations. This book was originally known as *Nevada Official Bicentennial Book.*

Note: All of the above titles are published or distributed by Nevada Publications, Box 15444, Las Vegas, Nevada 89114. Write for prices and descriptive brochure. There are other Comstock books still available. Grant H. Smith, *The History of The Comstock Lode, 1850-1920,* was published in 1943 by the Nevada State Bureau of Mines. This book is a modern reappraisal and summary of the Comstock Lode; the author carried his study well past the boom times.

Charles H. Shinn, *The Story of the Mine,* is an 1896 book recently reissued by the University of Nevada Press. It is a well organized contemporary account of the great Comstock Lode, with good material on the decline. Three excellent descriptive accounts by trained writers are Mark Twain's *Roughing It* (1872), Dan DeQuille's *The Big Bonanza,* (1876) and J. Ross Browne's *A Peep at Washoe* (1860) and *Washoe Revisited* (1863). All of these, reprinted in various forms many times, contain valuable observations of the life and boom times of Virginia City.

Effie Mona Mack's *Nevada...*, originally published in 1936, points out the Comstock Lode's significance to the entire western mining frontier. There is much concentration on political developments. Almost every phase of the Comstock Lode's history and development, including industrial, economic, social, musical, educational, and its institutions, have appeared in various books. See *Nevada, An Annotated Bibliography* (mentioned above) for specific citations.

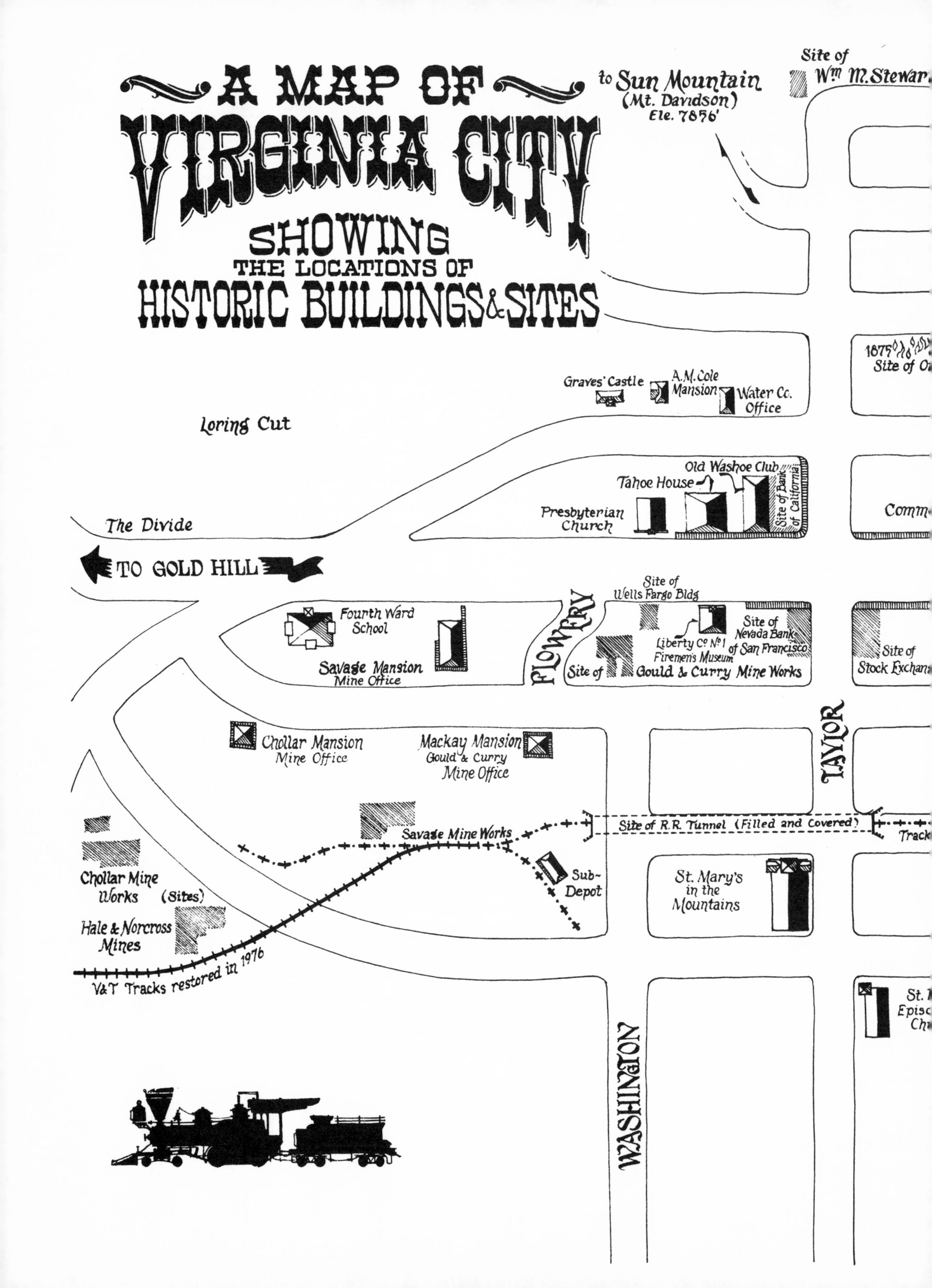

A MAP OF
VIRGINIA CITY
SHOWING
THE LOCATIONS OF
HISTORIC BUILDINGS & SITES
to Sun Mountain
(Mt. Davidson)
Ele. 7856'
Graves' Castle
A.M. Cole Mansion
Water Co. Office
Loring Cut
Old Washoe Club
Tahoe House
Presbyterian Church
Site of Bank of California
The Divide
TO GOLD HILL
Fourth Ward School
Savage Mansion
Mine Office
FLOWERY
Site of Wells Fargo Bldg
Liberty Co. No 1 Firemen's Museum
Site of Nevada Bank of San Francisco
Site of Gould & Curry Mine Works
TAYLOR
Chollar Mansion
Mine Office
Mackay Mansion
Gould & Curry
Mine Office
Site of R.R. Tunnel (Filled and Covered)
Savage Mine Works
Sub-Depot
St. Mary's in the Mountains
Chollar Mine Works (Sites)
Hale & Norcross Mines
V&T Tracks restored in 1976
WASHINGTON

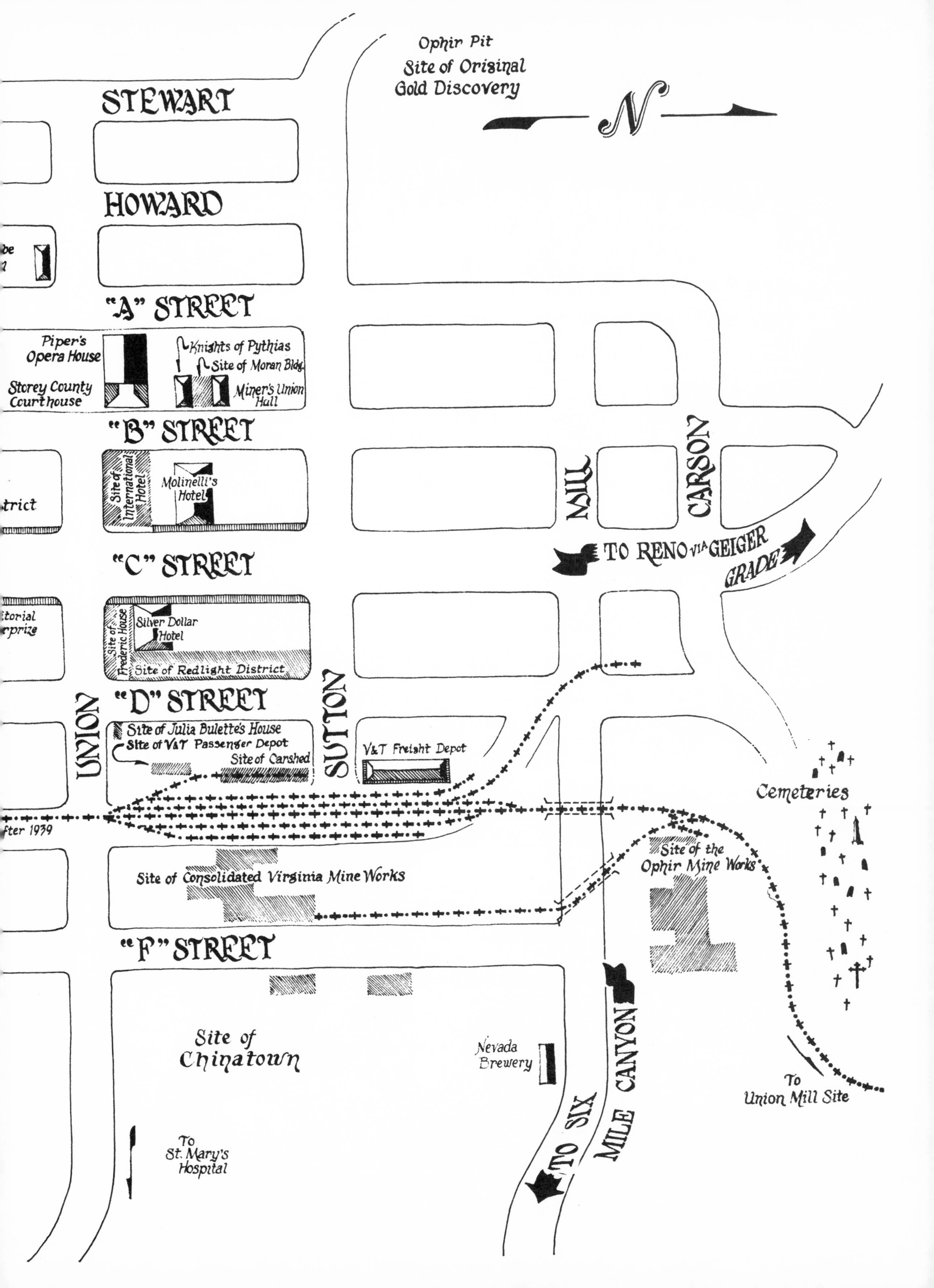

Ophir Pit
Site of Original
Gold Discovery
N
STEWART
HOWARD
"A" STREET
Piper's
Opera House
Storey County
Courthouse
Knights of Pythias
Site of Moran Bldg.
Miner's Union
Hall
"B" STREET
Site of
International
Hotel
Molinelli's
Hotel
MILL
CARSON
"C" STREET
TO RENO VIA GEIGER
GRADE
Site of
Frederic House
Silver Dollar
Hotel
Site of Redlight District
UNION
"D" STREET
SUTTON
Site of Julia Bulette's House
Site of V&T Passenger Depot
Site of Carshed
V&T Freight Depot
Cemeteries
Site of Consolidated Virginia Mine Works
Site of the
Ophir Mine Works
"F" STREET
Site of
Chinatown
Nevada
Brewery
TO SIX MILE CANYON
To
Union Mill Site
To
St. Mary's
Hospital

The Discoverers and Their Fates

In June, 1851, when John Reese's Mormon wagon train reached western Utah Territory to set up a trading post at Mormon Station, a teamster named James Finney was with the party. Through the years this man's name has been recorded as Finey, Fenimore, and even Ebenezer Fenemore, but he will always be remembered by his nickname of "Old Virginny."

Upon hearing that there were placer operations being worked in Gold Canyon, he immediately quit his job and became a miner, bringing the total number of men then working in the canyon to eighteen. Later that year he settled in the community known as Johntown, two miles from the mouth of Gold Canyon. His mining was very sporadic though, as Eliot Lord stated, "He only remained sober when he was too poor to buy whiskey and would never work longer than was necessary to obtain the means of filling his bottle."

On February 22, 1858, he decided to claim a ledge of rock on the east side of Sun Mountain, even filling out a location notice and hiding it in a crevice. He never worked the property but was always acknowledged to be the first locator of the "Virginia Lead" where Virginia City would one day stand. He was also instrumental in the discovery of the Gold Hill mines in January, 1859.

Henry Tompkins Paige Comstock was a Canadian fur trader, trapper, and general drifter until he happened to come to Gold Canyon in the mid-1850's. He took over the Grosh brothers' cabin and papers after their deaths; and while he could not fully determine that it was a silver vein they were working on, he did come to believe that there was a major orebody hidden somewhere in the area. He, too, was one of the first discoverers of the Gold Hill mines in 1859, but he also had the disconcerting habit of staking claims on practically any unoccupied ground.

In 1858 Patrick McLaughlin and Peter O'Riley were two of the Gold Canyon miners who had decided to set up placer operations in Six-Mile Canyon, running eastward from Sun Mountain. They also prospected Cedar Ravine until winter forced the abandonment

"OLD VIRGINIA" AT HIS ROCKER.

James Finney was among the earliest arrivals in Gold Canyon. He founded Johntown, was one of the discoverers of the Gold Hill mines, and was honored by having Virginia City named after him. Yet despite a decade of tedious efforts, he died in ignomy far from western Nevada.

of the canyon for the milder climate of Johntown.

When spring returned the two placer miners again began working their way up from Dutch Nick's, a rough saloon-restaurant in Six-Mile Canyon. They eventually panned a hefty amount of color at a little spring near the top of the canyon, prompting a decision to develop the site. On June 8, 1859, the first spadeful of dirt was turned into their hastily-erected placer equipment, thus opening the ground that would soon become known as the Ophir mine.

Almost immediately Henry Comstock arrived on the scene, stating that he had previously staked a 160-acre claim over the entire area. Besides that, he asserted, Old Virginny, Joseph Curly, James White, and William Hart had already filed a mining claim on the ground, plus Emanuel Penrod and himself owned nine-tenths of the water rights on the spring they were using. In return for a partnership in the mine, however, he would gladly see that all these conflicting claims were cleared up.

Whether any of the earlier claimants were legitimate, or if there even were any valid claims at all, is today unknown. But Penrod happily went along, paying $50 to Old Virginny, White, and Curly for a bill of sale. Only Hart did not receive any money as he had already left the vicinity. Comstock's participation in the purchase was limited to a blind horse, which he traded for the last 10 percent of water rights.

On about the 12th or 13th the placer ground revealed a quartz vein which continued to widen as it went down. This was the beginning of mining on the true Comstock Lode, named for a man whose only claim to partial ownership was a great deal of gall and one blind horse.

Total lode production has topped $400 million, but none of the discoverers retained possession of their claims long enough to realize any appreciable amount of money. Old Virginny was the first to trade off his portion of the original discovery, then for the next two years he eked out a small living by exchanging "feet" in various claims for food and liquor. On June 20, 1861, he was killed by a fall from a horse which fractured his skull.

Henry Comstock did a little better by selling his claims for $11,000 to James Walsh on August 12, 1859. He immediately made a bad investment with some of his new-found money when he bought a wife from a passing Mormon for $60, a horse, and a revolver. She immediately ran away whereupon Comstock offered a $100 reward for her return. The woman was brought back and the reward paid, but when she took off the second time he wisely decided to let the matter drop.

He later opened a store in Silver City and one in Carson, but when these also proved to be failures

H. T. P. COMSTOCK.

Comstock drifted away to other mining areas. The limelight quickly wore off as bystanders grew tired of listening to the often-repeated tale of how the great silver lode came to bear his name. On September 27, 1870, Henry Comstock used a revolver to commit suicide near Bozeman, Montana.

By the close of 1859 Peter O'Riley had sold his mining claims to John O. Earl for $40,000. At first he is reported to have invested the money wisely by building a stone hotel on C Street, but sold it and moved away. When he returned in 1867 he was broke and obsessed with the notion of driving a tunnel in a barren region of the Sierra. He started the project, living at a poverty level, but soon he began to converse with spirits and suffer delusions. A cave-in at the tunnel injured him severely, yet when he had recovered he fully intended to resume his mad excavating. Instead, he was committed to a mental institution at Woodbridge, California, where he died two years later.

Patrick McLaughlin sold his interest in the claims to George Hearst for $3,000, who eventually parlayed this into the fabulous Hearst fortune. McLaughlin had no such foresight, though, and he probably never saw that much money again in his life. He ended up employed as a cook for a group of miners in San Bernardino County, California, where he contracted a severe illness. When he died there in 1879 he was completely penniless.

None of these four men received any great amount for their part in the discovery, but such was often the case in western mining communities. Eliot Lord summed it up succinctly when he wrote, "In the discovery of rich ledges the element of chance largely enters."

Early Mining Law

When the first real mining discoveries were made along the Comstock Lode in 1859, there was little effective law in the area. As in other regions, miners drew up their own rules to govern each mining district. These usually proved sufficient until a more established system of laws could be instituted.

The original mining laws of both the Virginia and the Gold Hill mining districts have been previously published, but the laws of the Devil's Gate & China Town District, at the extreme southern end of the lode, were believed lost. Luckily an 1885 certified copy was found by Virginia City historian Douglas W. Walling, which is here published for the first time. It differs little from the original mining laws of other Comstock districts, but serves to illustrate what regulations the miners then deemed to be of importance.

Devil's Gate, showing the toll station in the foreground and Silver City beyond. This unique formation was one of the earliest landmarks in the area.

Mining Laws of Devils Gate & China Town District

By-Laws

At a meeting of the miners of Devils Gate and China Town District held at the Devils Gate on Sunday evening November 19th 1859 the following by laws were adopted.

Article 1st

This District shall be known as the Devils Gate and China Town Mining District, and shall be bounded as follows, to wit: Commencing at the Devils Gate and running in a westerly direction to the foot of the american flat; thence on a straight line to the eastern boundary of Eagle Valley and Washo District; thence following said line in a southeasterly direction to Rose's Dam, on Carson River, thence down said river to China Town, thence up the divide and along the western line of Virginia District to the head of Negro Ravine; thence in a straight line to the place of beginning.

Article 2d

All Quartz Veins of Gold or Silver hereafter located shall be two hundred feet on the lead including all its dips, angles, and spurs.

Article 3d

All discoverers of new veins shall be entitled to one additional claim for discovery.

Article 4th

All claims shall be designated by Stakes and Notices at each end.

Article 5th

All claims shall be worked to the amount of ten dollars — or three days work per month to each claim, but the owner can work to the amount of forty dollars as soon after location as he may see proper, which amount shall exempt him from working said claim for six months thereafter.

Article 6th

All claims shall be designated by a name and its locality particularly described.

Article 7

All claims shall be properly recorded within five days after location.

Article 8

All claims not worked according to the laws of the district shall be forfeited and subject to relocation.

Article 9

There shall be a *Recorder* elected to hold his office for the time of twelve months, who shall be entitled to fifty cents for each claim recorded.

Article 10

The Recorder shall keep in his own possession a well-bound book with all the laws of this District written therein, which shall at all times be subject to the inspection of the miners of this district.

Article 11

It shall be the duty of the Recorder to be on the ground located before recording the same.

Article 12

All notices of claims recorded under the Gold Hill laws, shall be transferred within twenty days after the adoption of the foregoing laws into this district, and shall be recorded free of charge.

Article 13

When a gold or silver vein is discovered and cannot be traced out at the time of its location, the owners of said ledge shall be entitled to all its dips and angles when found.

Article 14

Surface and all hill claims shall be one hundred feet square, and be designated by stakes and notices at each corner.

Article 15

All ravine and gulch claims shall be one hundred feet in length, and in width, extending from bank to bank, and be designated by a stake and notice at each end.

Article 16

All placer and gulch claims shall be worked within ten days after water can be had to work them.

Article 17

All disputes in regard to mining claims shall be decided by a miners court, which shall consist of a Justice whose duty it shall be to administer an oath or affirmation to witnesses and jurymen, the jury to consist of six or twelve persons as the Justice may agree and the majority of said jury shall decide the case.

On motion it was ordered that the foregoing laws be published in the Territorial Enterprise.

B. P. Brown
Prest.

P. C. Vanhorn
Secretary.

Law and Order

Early Mormon settlement and the establishment of Carson County over the area during the 1850's brought some measure of law and order to what was then western Utah Territory. By 1853, Justice of the Peace E. L. Barnard heard the first legal case brought to court in the area, then in 1855 Probate Judge Orson Hyde arrived to preside over all of Carson County. The following year Judge Drummond convened the First United States District Court, followed by Judge John Cradlebaugh's establishment of the Second Judicial District court in September, 1859.

However, the simple establishment of these various courts did not mean that such a system actually worked. When the "Rush to Washoe" began, with thousands of people flocking to the sparsely-settled region around the Comstock Lode, the legal apparatus was totally unable to cope with the increased criminal element. Myron Angel summed it up succinctly when he wrote, "The judicial administration was rather a struggle, with indecisive results, to assert law and order in a community where much of irregularity was prevalent."

Vigilante groups first sprang up in the vicinity of Genoa and Carson City, with one such 1858 group

"The 601"

eventually evolving into the Law and Order political party. The fact that the area was hundreds of miles removed from the Utah Territorial capitol at Salt Lake City, plus the departure of many of the Mormons from Carson County in 1857, forced local residents to take the law into their own hands to eliminate some of the true "hardcases" in the area.

Sam Brown was perhaps the most notorious cold-blooded killer in the entire region. In February, 1859, he murdered William Bilboa on a Carson City street, stabbed Homer Woodruff to death in Virginia City 11 months later, and cut the heart out of a man named McKenzie in Virginia City early in 1861. He was known to have committed at least six more murders elsewhere, and was suspected of numerous additional homicides in the Virginia City-Carson City area. When law officers continued to ignore his terrible crimes, easy-going Henry Van Sickle proceeded to "execute" Brown with a shotgun.

By itself, Virginia City was remarkably well-regulated during its early years. There were no infamous fast-shooting marshals or sheriffs needed to keep the peace, for there were few true outlaws on the Comstock. Even with the sudden influx of thousands of people, there were only five murders there in 1860, one in 1861, and three in 1862.

The following year things got a little out of hand. Suddenly from mid-summer on, reports of brawls, murders, robberies, and gunfights were an almost daily occurrence. Two policemen were killed attempting to arrest a drunk; prostitutes in the red-light district did away with two more men; and a fight between two rival fire companies caused the death of still another man. All told there were 13 homicides that year, equal to the total number occurring between 1859 and 1862. Never again would violence be as severe on the Comstock, for in the entire decade from 1870 to 1880, when population hit its all-time high, there were only 14 homicides.

When a particularly obnoxious man could not be dealt with legally, a quiet vigilance committee known as the "601" would convene. The offender was usually given a specific charge to permanently leave the vicinity. If that warning was ignored, he was soon found lynched in some convenient spot. Such was the case with George Kirk, who returned to Virginia City in 1871 after being warned away once. He was found hanging from the headframe of the Sierra Nevada mine with a note reading "601" pinned to his shirt. It took very few of these hangings before a warning from the "601" was sufficient to send a man hightailing to another part of the country.

With the 400-odd murders which occurred in Nevada during the years 1851-1880, only eight persons were legally executed for their crimes, 23 were sent to the State Prison, and 29 were acquitted. One murderer was simply found guilty of assault, and merely fined. It is therefore no wonder that private citizens and vigilance committees hanged 13 murderers during this period — it is only remarkable that they did not account for more.

W. C. Frank, alias Frank Dow, was a Nevada stage robber killed in 1880.

"HOLD UP YOUR HANDS!"

This typical armed westerner of the 1880's brandishes a Colt single-action revolver and a Springfield trapdoor rifle.

One of the most famous Comstock outlaws was "Big Jack" Davis. In public he was a respectable Virginia City businessman, but in private he headed a gang of outlaws who would make history. At a time when enormously high shipping rates were being charged by express companies, highwaymen robbing the stages were simply thought of by most people as thieves robbing thieves. Big Jack's gang found it quite easy to stop a Pioneer Line stagecoach, remove the Wells Fargo box, and escape into the sage. Wells Fargo did not take kindly to these actions, countering by disguising guards as women with shotguns under their skirts, sending treasure coaches out in tandem, and hiring messengers who were known to shoot first and ask questions later. When the completion of the Virginia & Truckee Railroad enabled Wells Fargo to send treasure shipments out of Virginia City in a specially-built railroad car, Big Jack decided to look around for another type of outlawry.

On November 4, 1870, only 18 months after the transcontinental railroad was completed, Big Jack and his gang stopped the Central Pacific eastbound train at Verdi, ten miles west of Reno. They removed $41,000 in gold, thereby carving a niche in American history by pulling off the first train robbery in the Far West. Local sheriffs and Wells Fargo detectives soon rounded up the entire bunch, with Davis and most of his cohorts receiving sentences in the State Prison.

Big Jack aided in quelling a prison break a few years later, for which he was subsequently pardoned. He swore never to engage in highway robbery again, and for a time it seemed that he would keep his word. Then one night the Eureka-Tybo stage in eastern Nevada was stopped by three masked men who demanded that the messengers "throw down the box." However, the express guards that night were Eugene Blair and Jimmy Brown, who had shot their way out of more attempted robberies than any other express guards in Nevada. Brown's double-barrelled shotgun roared from the coach, and Big Jack Davis was dead.

All in all, Virginia City was much more peaceful than such other western mining towns as Tombstone, Pioche, or Bodie. There was indeed a small element of serious lawbreakers, which sometimes necessitated citizen action in lieu of the often-ineffectual legal system, but there was never any serious rampage of crime. The brand of outlaws and peace officers portrayed in novels and on television simply did not exist on the Comstock, a place where culture and good manners were more highly admired than notoriety.

The Pioneer Stage Driver

by Charley Rhoades

In the 1860's when rich treasure shipments were still being sent from Virginia City via flimsy stage-coaches, highway robbery became a fairly common occurrence on the steep mountain roads. Wells Fargo was then charging rates many people considered exhorbitant, as well as guaranteeing full monetary replacement of any shipment they did not deliver safely, so the robberies became a light-hearted subject with the general public.

This song of one of Wells Fargo's most-robbed stage drivers became very popular in Virginia City during the early 1860's, typifying the attitude of the times. However, Joe Goodman later wrote, "Poor Baldy Green...was held up so often that he was finally discharged, either from a superstitious belief in his bad luck or a suspicion of his fidelity."

I'm going to tell a story,
And I'll tell it in my song,
I hope that it will please you,
And I won't detain you long;
It's about one of the old boys,
So gallas and so fine,
He used to carry mails,
On the Pioneer line.

He was such a favorite
Wherever he was seen,
He was known about Virginia
By the name of Baldy Green;
Oh! he swung a whip so graceful,
For he was bound to shine,
As a high-toned driver
On the Pioneer line.

As he was driving up one night,
As lively as a coon,
He saw four men jump in the road,
By the pale light of the moon;
One sprang for his leaders
While another his gun he cocks,
Saying, "Baldy I hate to trouble you,
But pass me out that box."

When Baldy heard him say these words,
He opened wide his eyes,
He didn't know what in the devil to do,
It took him by surprise;
But he reached down in the boot,
Saying, "Take it, sir, with pleasure,"
And out into the middle of the road,
Went Wells & Fargo's treasure.

Now when they'd got the treasure-box,
They seem'd quite satisfied, —
The man that held the horses,
Politely stepped aside,
Saying, "Baldy, we've got what we want,
Just drive along your team,"
And he made the quickest time
To Silver City ever seen.

If you say greenbacks to Baldy now,
It makes him feel so sore,
It's the first time he was ever stopped,
And he's drove that road before;
But they play'd four hands against his one,
And shot guns was their game,
And if I had been in Baldy's place,
I'd have passed it out the same.

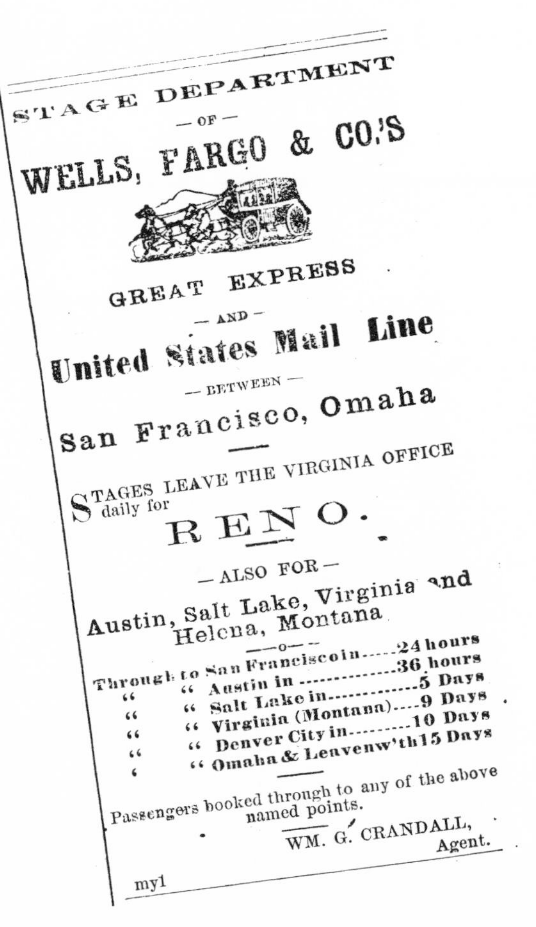

DANGEROUS BOULDERS.

Square Set Timbering

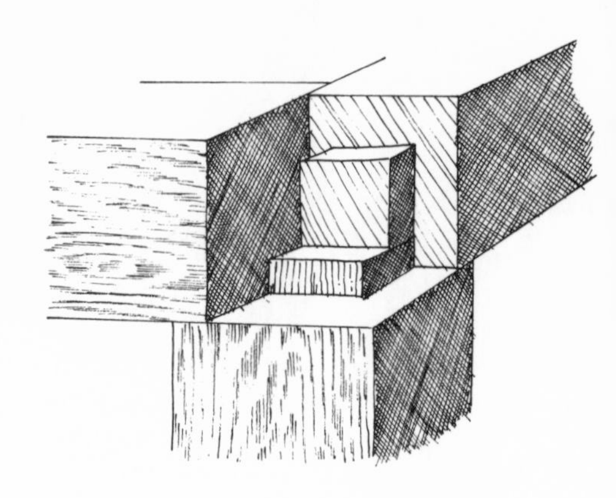

Born in Germany in 1832, Philipp Deidesheimer came to California in 1851 where he eventually became superintendent of a mine at Georgetown. By the fall of 1860 Virginia City's Ophir mine had encountered an orebody so large that no conventional method of mine timbering could hold the ground if it were removed. Deidesheimer's reputation had become well known by this time, so in desperation he was summoned by W. F. Babcock, one of the Ophir's directors, before a major cave-in occurred.

Deidesheimer agreed to look into the problem, arriving in Virginia City on November 8. It took him less than six weeks to study the situation, conduct some experiments, and invent the totally-new system of timbering known as square set. The Ophir immediately put it to use on its orebody, and by February, 1861, had mined out a stope 65 feet wide which was entirely supported by this timbering.

Other Comstock mine owners and superintendents were invited to view the timbering, quickly adapting it to their own operations. Deidesheimer refused to patent his invention, which he could easily have done, but instead he chose to let anyone use it to increase safety in the mines. As a reward the Ophir put him in charge of the mine with the title of Mining Engineer, but by 1863 he was superintendent of the Burning Moscow mine and was involved in a ferocious legal battle with the Ophir.

For all his wisdom concerning the Comstock Lode, Deidesheimer was one of the few superintendents who did not realize a great deal of money there. In fact, after making a ridiculous claim in December, 1874, that the Big Bonanza would eventually yield $1.5 billion, he proceeded to invest every dollar he had into buying stock on margin. When the stock market crashed early in 1875, he was forced into

bankruptcy with liabilities of $534,600, but William Sharon returned him to the position of superintendent of the Ophir mine later that year.

In the early 1880's Deidesheimer left Virginia City to become one of the owners of the Young America mine in Sierra City, California, where a five-year period of bonanza saw him comfortably well fixed. While he lived to an old age he never became truly wealthy from mining, although it was his invention more than any other single mining innovation that enabled the deep mines and stopes of the Comstock, including that of the Big Bonanza, to produce their many millions in bullion.

At the timber shop of the Arizona Comstock mine, various sizes of timbers were sawn into square set, as shown by the workman at right using a belt-driven saw. Deidesheimer's system of square set timbering is illustrated.

The Carson River Mills

The Ophir mine was not only the site of the discovery of the Comstock Lode in 1859, it was also the first mine to ship ore for reduction. The Mexican mine followed soon thereafter, with both operations being forced to freight their ore over the Sierra to California where the nearest mills were located. It was not long before mine owners realized that these transportation costs would not only cut deeply into their profits, but would also preclude the shipment of low-grade ore.

The Carson River was the nearest source of running water, a commodity necessary to power most types of quartz reduction works. The first operation of this sort on the river was a small mill built in 1860 at a site near Empire City. It was later enlarged and known as the Silver State mill. By the mid-1860's Empire City had become a prominent milling center, home to the Mexican, Mead's, and Baldwin's mills. Numerous other quartz mills were constructed downstream until the canyon from Empire to Dayton was filled with noisy reduction works, most on the north side of the Carson River.

East from Empire were the Brunswick and Blue Canyon mills, the latter renamed Copper Canyon mill then finally known as the Yerington Smelter. The Merrimac mill, built in 1861, was also located in this vicinity. It acquired its own railroad unloading facilities, known as Merrimac Siding, when the V&T RR was constructed in 1869.

Still further east was the 16-stamp Vivian mill, built in 1862 on the river's south bank. Next was the Stewart & Hennings quartz mill, which by 1863 had been renamed the Zephyr Flat and was later called the Santiago. It was only a 12-stamp operation, but was powered by a seven-foot turbine water wheel weighing 7,000 pounds.

Further downstream was the Eureka mill, which in 1862 had 20 stamps and four arrastras. When the V&T was built nearby, a very short mining railroad was constructed to haul ore from bins along the V&T's right-of-way to the mill itself. Immediately below it was the 20-stamp San Francisco mill, while its neighbor to the east was the Franklin mill of ten stamps and two arrastras. The Baron Company's mill was situated on the south side of the river here, but it was a fairly short-lived operation which used arrastras only.

Sproul's mill was next downstream, followed by the Carson River quartz mill, later renamed the Woodworth. Five minor mills occupied the distance between the last named and Dayton, being the Aurora, Keller, Solomon & Jacobs, and Dayton mills. The Mineral Rapids mill, owned by the Imperial Mining Company, was built just outside of Dayton. It was later renamed the Rock Point mill, then the Nevada Reduction Works, remaining in use until destroyed by fire in 1909. Downstream from Dayton four additional mills worked Comstock ore. They

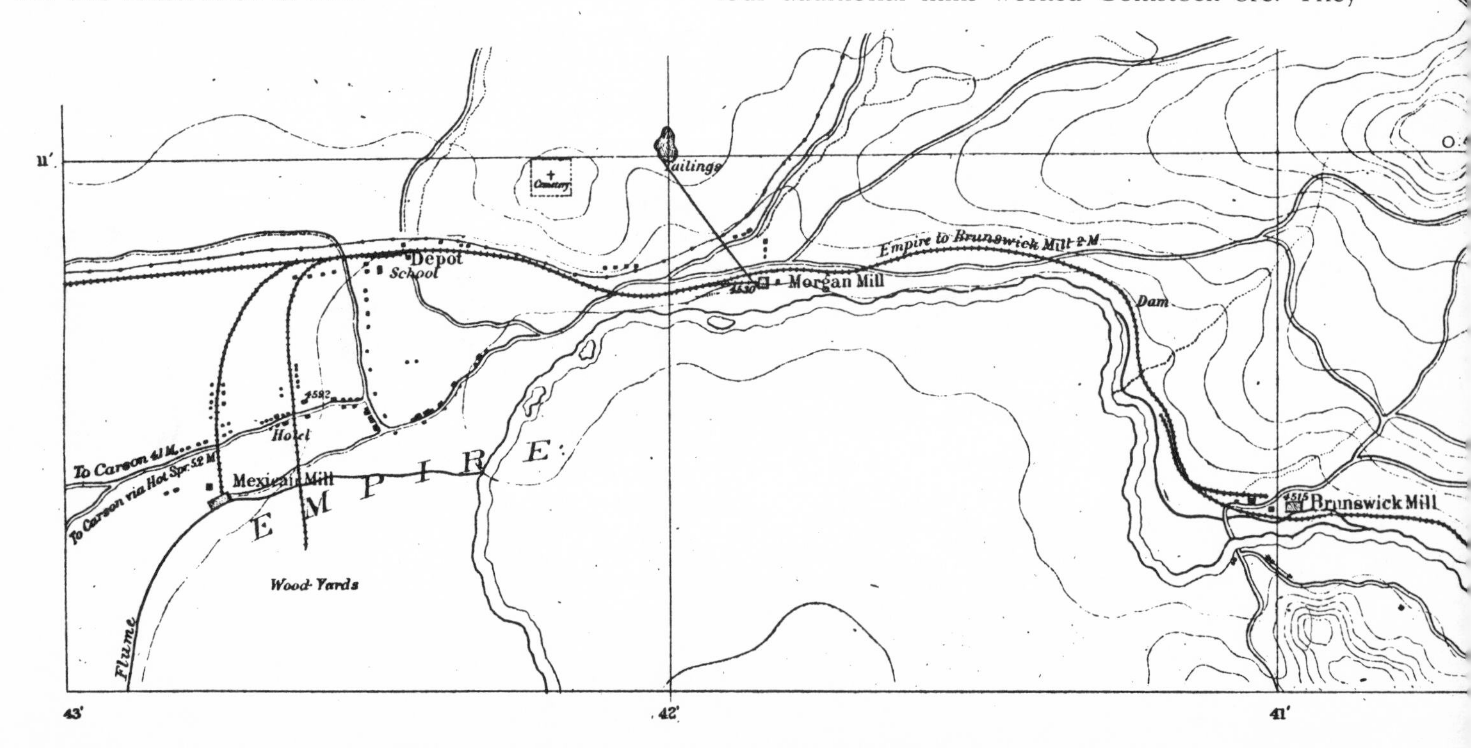

This westbound Virginia & Truckee RR train is approaching Empire City. From here to the Dayton area both banks of the Carson River were sites of the major mills which reduced Comstock ore.

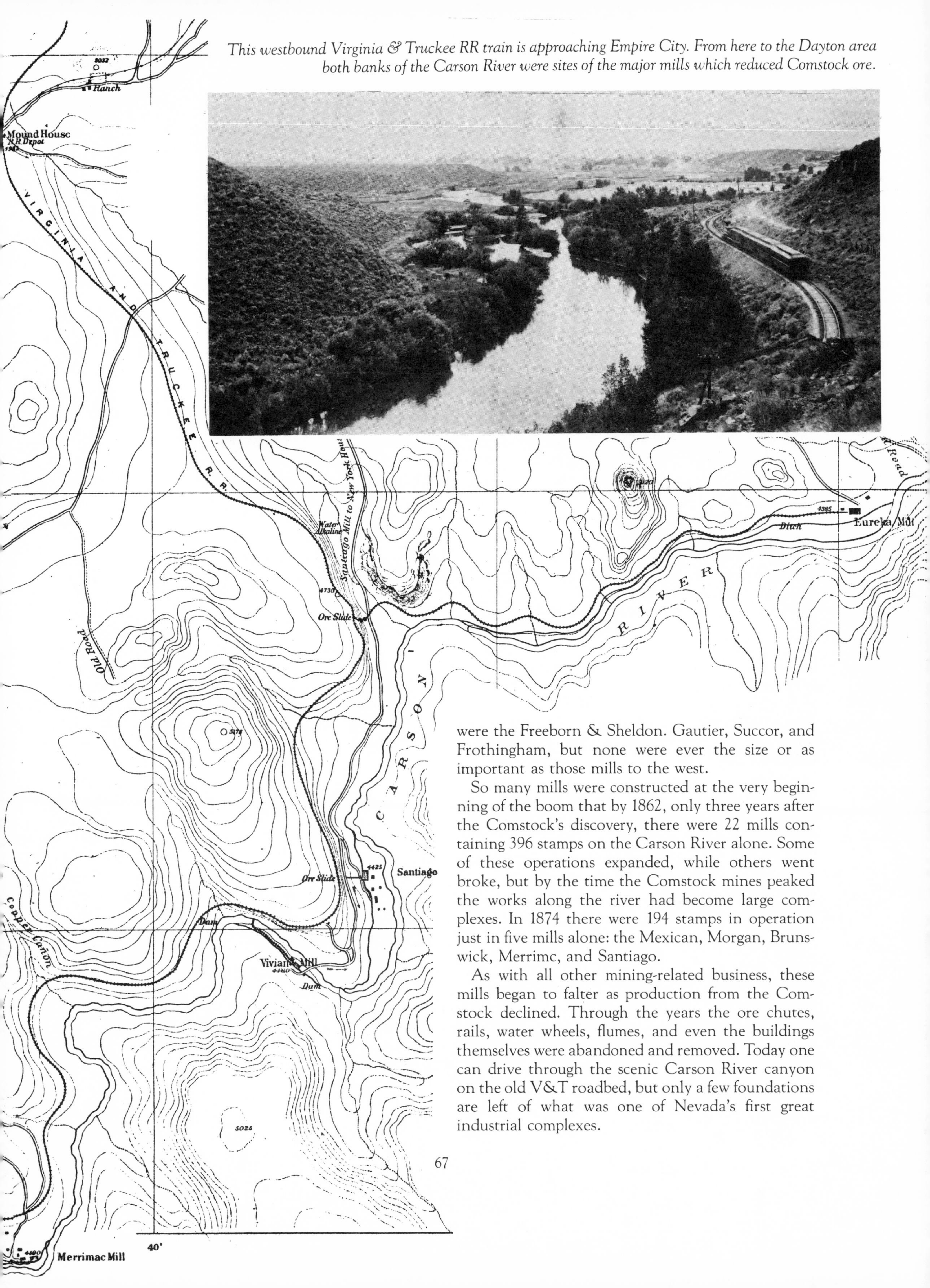

were the Freeborn & Sheldon. Gautier, Succor, and Frothingham, but none were ever the size or as important as those mills to the west.

So many mills were constructed at the very beginning of the boom that by 1862, only three years after the Comstock's discovery, there were 22 mills containing 396 stamps on the Carson River alone. Some of these operations expanded, while others went broke, but by the time the Comstock mines peaked the works along the river had become large complexes. In 1874 there were 194 stamps in operation just in five mills alone: the Mexican, Morgan, Brunswick, Merrimc, and Santiago.

As with all other mining-related business, these mills began to falter as production from the Comstock declined. Through the years the ore chutes, rails, water wheels, flumes, and even the buildings themselves were abandoned and removed. Today one can drive through the scenic Carson River canyon on the old V&T roadbed, but only a few foundations are left of what was one of Nevada's first great industrial complexes.

Mark Twain

AS CITY EDITOR.

When James W. Nye was appointed Governor of the newly-created Nevada Territory, his friend Orion Clemens received a commission five days later naming him Territorial Secretary. At the time Orion's younger brother, Samuel, had given up his career as a riverboat pilot and was artfully dodging his ill-advised enlistment in an irregular Confederate guerilla outfit known as the Marion Rangers. When Orion offered him a position as personal secretary, Sam jumped at the chance to head west with him. Together they boarded an overland stagecoach, arriving in Carson City at the end of an arduous 20-day journey.

Orion immediately became involved in the myriad duties necessary to organize and administer the new government, leaving Sam to fend for himself. After a short time spent exploring the Carson area, he contracted mining fever and set off to make his fortune. Sam's first venture entailed walking nearly 200 miles to Unionville, where he arrived in a snowstorm. His four-man party quickly built a rough cabin, then commenced prospecting and staking claims as rapidly as possible. They never found even a single specimen of high-grade ore, returning to Carson discouraged and broke after only a few weeks.

Still bitten by the mining bug, Sam soon set off for Aurora where he again went broke without finding one promising lead. He later wrote, "I went to work as a common laborer in a quartz mill at ten dollars a week and board."

During this fruitless stay in Aurora, Sam wrote some humorous letters to the Virginia City *Territorial Enterprise*, and was always surprised when they appeared in print. "My good opinion of the editors

INNOCENT DREAMS.

Mark Twain's book, Roughing It, *is amply illustrated with fascinating line drawings showing life in the Far West. In "Innocent Dreams" Twain is still in his Missouri hometown contemplating adventures which might be encountered enroute to his frontier destination, Nevada Territory. He dreams of meeting Indians, buffalo, miners, along with steamboats and wagons. "Envious contemplations" (opposite) depicts Twain casting his eyes on the editor's job (reporter) for the Virginia City newspaper.*

had steadily declined," he later wrote, "for it seemed to me that they might have found something better to fill up with than my literature." However, when an offer of $25 a week was tendered for him to come to work for the newspaper, Sam quickly headed for Virginia City.

The Comstock has never had a more outlandish writer than Clemens proved to be. Soon after his arrival in September, 1862, he began poking fun at everyone from the Governor to the most respected businessman. His stories also told of blatantly false massacres, impossible scientific discoveries, and highly inflated mining strikes. His technique of either coloring true stories to make them sound more exciting, or fabricating news events out of whole cloth when times were a little slow, is a Comstock tradition which has endured for more than a century.

Unfortunately, very few issues of the *Enterprise* exist prior to the great fire of 1875. It is known that Clemen's first journalistic endeavors were by-lined "Josh," and that a further series of humorous letters were signed "Professor Personal Pronoun." It was not until January, 1863, that he bagan using the by-line "Mark Twain," which is believed to have originated with his custom of ordering two drinks at a time to be chalked up on the slate used to tally bar tabs in a local saloon. His given name was quickly forgotten, as he became known both personally and in print by his pseudonym.

The articles he wrote in Virginia City were often picked up by other Nevada and California papers. It wasn't long before he was being asked to write pieces for such eminent publications as San Francisco's *Golden Era*. He hob-nobbed with the gentry and lesser classes alike, partook of every social event he was invited to, and insulted or poked fun at everyone. In short, as he once wrote home, "I am proud to say I am the most conceited ass in the Territory."

But Twain could not keep insulting people wantonly and continue to get away with it. In May, 1864, he severely slandered the women of Carson City who had put on a fancy dress ball to raise money for the Sanitary Fund, a Civil War version of the Red Cross. While the effects of this error were still being felt, he proceeded to belittle the rival Virginia City *Daily Union* over their lack of contributions to this same fund. They immediately responded by calling Twain "a liar, a poltroon and a puppy."

The *Union's* James Laird took the position of champion for his newspaper. In one day six letters were exchanged between the two, with Twain challenging Laird to a duel under the prevailing codes. Two days later the correspondence resumed, with the *Enterprise* publishing both men's letters to keep the public well informed. Soon newspapers throughout Nevada and

ENVIOUS CONTEMPLATIONS.

California were commenting on the pending duel, and the occasion had suddenly gotten so far out of hand that neither party could honorably retreat.

It is reasonable to assume now that Twain was prompted not by fear of the duel itself, but rather by possible repercussions of Nevada's strong anti-dueling statute. Any any rate, he borrowed $200 from his brother before leaving Virginia City for San Francisco on May 29. His refusal to engage Lair on the field of honor was soon forgotten in the crush of everyday activity, so when he returned on a lecture tour some years later he was welcomed as a long-lost son.

While the events and lifestyle peculiar to the Comstock did much to shape Twain's writing style, and gave him the *nom de plume* he would make world famous, the items he contributed to the *Enterprise* were by no means his first literary attempts. Writing as Sam Clemens, he had published an article in the Boston *Carpet Bag* as early as 1852, and had authored the Thomas Jefferson Snodgrass letters which ran in the Keokuk *Saturday Post* four years later. However, the heady and flamboyant two years he spent in Virginia City undoubtedly provided him with the opportunity to practice and enlarge upon the style of writing which would soon make him the most widely-known American humorist.

When he later wrote *Roughing It,* Twain's own version of his adventures in Nevada Territory, he commented on his departure from Virginia City. "It is not without regret that I took a last look at the tiny flag...fluttering like a lady's handkerchief from the topmost peak of Virginia's roofs, and felt that doubtless I was bidding a permanent farewell to a city which had afforded me the most vigorous enjoyment of life I had ever experienced."

The Territorial Enterprise

The distinction of being the first newspaper in what is now Nevada must fall to the mid-1850's holographic "newsletter" entitled *Gold Canyon Switch.* But the first hand-set, machine-printed newspaper was the December 18, 1858, issue of the *Territorial Enterprise,* published in Genoa by W. L. Jernegan and A. James. A year later, on November 9, 1859, the weekly paper was moved to Carson City, closer to the area of greatest activity. Finally in October, 1860, it was relocated a third time to Virginia City, where it became a daily a year later.

Ownership changed hands many times in the early years, but the *Enterprise* truly became one of the most influential newspapers in the West during the years 1861 to 1874, when Joseph T. Goodman was proprietor. It was under his leadership that Sam Clemens began to develop his style of humor while using the *nom de plume* Mark Twain. At the same time William Wright, another humorist writing as Dan de Quille, was perfecting the capacity for local color which would later enable him to write the very important Comstock history entitled *The Big Bonanza.*

With Goodman at the helm and such notable writers on the staff, the *Enterprise* is said to have made a profit of $1,000 a day, although that figure seems quite improbable. However, it did generate enough income to warrant the paper's relocation to a frame building on the site of today's Silver Queen casino, then later in 1863 its own two-story brick building was constructed a little farther south on C Street.

Throughout the early 1860's and 1870's the *Enterprise* delighted in printing articles which would undoubtedly result in lawsuits if published today. No punches were pulled in promoting such events as stage productions, new mining discoveries, or the patronage of a particular saloon. In return, the persons so "plugged" would often respond with gratis theatre passes, shares in mines, or a case of the author's favorite liquor. By the same token when the paper's staff felt that a wrong had been done, either real or imagined, the *Enterprise* could be so thoroughly devastating that politicians, businessmen, and financiers could suffer irreparable reverses.

Such was the power of this paper that William Sharon, whom the *Enterprise* had helped to defeat in his 1872 bid for a U.S. Senate seat, finally had to purchase the newspaper to insure his election when he again ran two years later. With Mark Twain having departed a decade earlier, and Goodman's dislike of Sharon causing his removal from the staff, the *Enterprise* lost much of its zest during this time.

The rise of the Bonanza Firm of Mackay, Fair, Flood, and O'Brien challenged the stranglehold the Bank of California had on the Comstock. Sharon had a newspaper and the Bonanza Kings did not, so they set about buying a partnership in the *Enterprise.* With these two conflicting parties in control, the paper lost even more of its forthright appeal.

By 1893, with total cirulation down to 350 copies, the paper folded. It was reactivated a year later, but with the continued decline of the mines it shut down again in 1916 and was absorbed by the *Virginia Evening Chronicle.* The paper's legendary name still appeared in small type on the masthead of the *Virginia City News* until Lucius Beebe and Charles Clegg once again began publishing the *Enterprise* in 1951 from its original building on C Street.

Immediately the reactivated weekly *Territorial Enterprise* began attracting attention nationwide. Writing of the Mark Twain and Dan de Quille style filled the pages, while ads were solicited from well-known restaurants, hotels, and businesses from New York to California. More than anything else, the *Enterprise* was responsible for the huge increase in tourism which the Comstock is still enoying today.

The paper once again folded in the mid-1960's, after Beebe's death. Clegg moved to his California residence, where he died in 1979. However, a legal battle over ownership of the *Enterprise* name raged in 1980, indicating that someone may soon resume publication.

Some 17 separate newspapers were published at various times in Virginia City between 1860 and 1880, yet the distinctive style and editorial policy of the *Enterprise* kept it from ever being surpassed. Much more would be known about the Comstock's early history if all of the first issues were available,

but the fire of 1875 destroyed the only complete files. A few scattered editions dated in the 1860's and the brick office building are all that remain of the early years of the *Territorial Enterprise*, the newspaper that not only served to make the Comstock known worldwide but also helped to foster American journalism and literature as well.

Composing room of the Territorial Enterprise *in the 1890's (above). The newspaper's chief competitor at the time was the* Virginia Evening Chronicle, *whose composing room is shown in this 1896 photo below.*

Forts and the Military on the Comstock

On March 2, 1861, only one month prior to the beginning of the Civil War, Nevada Territory was created. Three years later, on October 31, 1864, this territory became the 36th state in the Union. Thus while the territory was in existence the shadow of this enormous conflict hung over the region, giving rise to the official state motto — "Battle Born."

Local battles had begun much earlier, though. On May 7, 1860, a small party of Paiutes attacked and burned Williams' Station on the Carson River, leaving four white men dead. When the news reached the Comstock the only thought was for retaliation. Accordingly, 105 men from Virginia City, Silver City, Carson, and Genoa marched out two days later to do battle with the Paiutes. An Indian ambush on the Truckee River, some two miles south of Pyramid Lake, completely routed the volunteer militia. Forty-six men were slain, including Major Ormsby who had been the unofficial leader of the expedition.

Anger turned to panic among the white population as a major Indian uprising was feared. Women and children were barricaded in a house in Carson City, Warren Wasson's stone cabin in Genoa was converted into a blockhouse, and a partially- completed stone hotel in Virginia City was garrisoned and renamed Fort Riley. The residents of Silver City constructed the first true fort on the Comstock by erecting a low stone redoubt on top of Devil's Gate. This was staffed by armed civilians and boasted a home-made cannon of wood banded with iron.

The Paiutes did not attack the settlements, as had been feared. Instead, volunteers from all over California arrived, along with 500 extra muskets and cases of ammunition. The Washoe Regiment, consisting of eight companies of infantry and six companies of cavalry, marched out of Virginia City on May 24 under the command of veteran Indian fighter Colonel John C. Hays. Along the march they were joined by 754 men of the U.S. Army who had hurried over from California with two howitzers.

The Second Battle of Pyramid Lake occurred very near the scene of the first, but the result was much different. This time the heavily-outnumbered Indians suffered between 40 and 50 dead and were driven into the desert hills east of the lake. The whites had only three dead and five wounded, although one of the dead was Captain Storey of the Virginia Rifles, for whom Storey County was later named.

Sporadic Paiute "outrages" would occur infrequently for many years still, but never again would they gather in such numbers to fight against the whites. It was also fortunate that the Silver City volunteers were never forced to defend the small fort on Devil's Gate. After the Indian scare had died down, a local citizen took the wooden cannon into the hills and fired it with a fuse. The big gun exploded in a rain of wood and iron shrapnel, which would certainly have killed a number of men if it has been fired while within the little fort.

When the Washoe Regiment was disbanded, two companies of infantry and one of dragoons were ordered to remain in Nevada to establish a fort on the Carson River, 30 miles east of Virginia City. While little more than a collection of rude adobe buildings, the outpost was officially named Fort Churchill on August 25.

Since before the start of the Civil War, the South had looked longingly at the Comstock silver mines. David S. Terry, previously a California Supreme Court Judge and the known murderer of U.S. Senator Broderick, had been among the first to arrive in Virginia City. He supposedly had with him a commission from Jefferson Davis which would grant him the Governorship of the area when it was safely in the hands of the rebels. He did not reckon with the power of William Stewart, though, nor with the fact that majority of the men on the Comstock were vehemently pro-Union. After a protracted struggle that nearly became a pitched battle, Stewart succeeded in legal maneuverings which forced Terry to withdraw from the region.

A small secret society of pro-Confederate sympathizers, known as the Knights of the Golden Circle, were present on the Comstock during the war, but they were never able to mke any headway against the nearly-unanimous pro-Union sentiments. Men who did speak out too loudly against Washington and for Richmond were often hauled to Fort Churchill in

Gold Hill in the 1860's featured Fort Homestead on the hill to the left.

irons, then forced to march around the parade gound for hours carrying heavy sandbags.

Union recruiting drives on the Comstock commenced soon after Fort Sumter was fired upon, though the first volunteers were assigned to a California militia. It was not until 1863 that Nevada was allowed to raise its own units, the first being Company B of the 1st Nevada Territorial Cavalry Volunteers at Gold Hill. Company A was soon founded at Silver City, then these first two units were detached to Camp Douglas, Utah, to relieve regular troops stationed there and to keep an eye on the Mormons. Four additional cavalry and six infantry companies were also raised in western Nevada.

Colonel P. E. Connor and his 3rd California Volunteers took command of Fort Churchill in 1863, again to relieve federal toops for service back east. When that fort became overcrowded by volunteers in the summer of 1864, an additional fort was established on a ridge overlooking Gold Hill. Known as Fort Homestead because the site was leased from the Homestead Mining Co., it was more of a patriotic rallying point than a true military compound, although it did boast at least one cannon.

With the end of the Civil War and the peaceful nature of the local Indians, the Army abandoned Fort Churchill in late 1869 but Fort Homestead became a public meeting place and picnic spot, sporting a 6-pounder and 32-pounder cannons which had been purchased by public subscription. The site was used for events such as dances and political gatherings where cannon salutes would boom out on special occasions, until nearby residents began to complain of broken windows and roof damage. The salutes were first discontinued, then the guns were removed in 1874. Gradually the buildings fell into ruin, until today no traces remain of the original compound.

There are no forts left in Nevada now, but the volunteer militia continued to grow. Today's National Guard owes its formation to the first cavalrymen who formed Company B in 1863. Or perhaps it could even be said their beginnings were in the band of volunteer Indian fighters who engaged the Paiutes in battle at Pyramid Lake. Either way, the Comstock provided the foundation for the mobile, highly-effective Army and Air units of the present Nevada National Guard.

Prostitution

As in all early-day Western communities, prostitution was a ubiquitous and accepted facet of local society. Most of the men who flocked to the first mining discoveries were single and very far from wherever they called home. The ratio of men to women was consistently off-balance, usually remaining so for many years following the original boom, and Virginia City was no exception. A census conducted in August, 1860, showed 2,390 men in Virginia City and only 118 women, or a ratio of more than 20 to 1.

While never officially legalized by ordinance or statute, prostitution was nonetheless regulated to an extent. In Virginia City there were three main districts where this activity was allowed — the main red-light district on North D Street, the rude bordellos of Chinatown which housed only Oriental women, and the infamous "Barbary Coast" area of South C Street. The only licensing required, however, was for those establishments which sold beer or liquor.

Known as "hurdies," "fallen women," or the "fair but frail," prostitutes occupied social strata according to their clientele and where they worked. The best class lived in quite fancy brothels, often with parlors containing a piano played by a paid musician which gave rise to the term "parlor house." Such places were used as much for their social as their sexual atmosphere, though the women employed there were of the best caliber and often charged $10 to $20 per customer.

Next down the social ladder were the single prostitutes who lived alone in rented cabins, such as Julia Bulette, the most famous of all Comstock prostitutes. These women were usually quiet, discreet, of "good" character, and often allowed only one customer per night.

Below them, in descending order of social class, were the women employed in the disreputable brothels, those who worked the back rooms of the saloons and dance halls of the "Barbary Coast," and the Oriental women sold into slavery who occupied the Chinatown brothels. This last category were the worst off, usually having no choice as to occupation, taking many customers per night at $1 each, and being forced to turn over all of their earnings to their masters.

Alcoholism and drug addiction were quite common among the lower-class prostitutes but the rate of social diseases was relatively low, probably owing to frequent medical checks by most of the women. Only in the half dozen or so saloons comprising the "Barbary Coast" was there any real atmosphere of underworld activity, and here it was as easy to be served a "Mickey Finn" as an honest drink.

By and large, prostitution was carried on in Virginia City quietly and without much notice. There were the occasional acts of violence, and local newspapers bowed to "respectable" pressure once in awhile to urge abolition of the red-light district and the Barbary Coast, but as long as there were men with money around the business flourished. When the population began to dwindle as the mines cut back or shut down, the "fair but frail" moved on to more lively towns until by the 1940's there were only a handful left. A rare few married and settled down, but many of the "girls" working the "line" at Rawhide, Goldfield, and Tonopah had previously occupied cribs on D Street.

In 1947 prostitution was finally outlawed in Virginia City, although two decades later the County Commissioners made history by passing the first county ordinance in the U.S. actually legalizing this business. They did, however, relegate it to the extreme northern portion of the county, many miles from the Comstock Lode.

Julia Bulette, the Legend and the Woman . . . .

On the morning of January 20, 1867, the well-liked prostitute known as Julia C. Bulette was found murdered in the small frame house she rented on D Street. As she was an honorary member of Virginia Engine Co. No. 1, the deeply-shocked firemen turned out *en masse* to bury her, then a determined search was launched for her murderer.

On May 26 a Frenchman, John Millian, was charged with that crime. So much evidence had been collected against him that when his trial finally began on July 2, the outcome was practically a foregone conclusion. The verdict was guilty, and Millian was publicly hanged on April 24, 1868, while some 3,000 persons looked on.

Storey County District Attorney Bishop summarized the situation. "Although this community has, in times past, seen blood run like water, yet in most cases there was some cause brought forward in justification of the deed, some pretext. But on the morning of the 20th of January last, this community, so hardened by previous deeds of blood, was struck dumb with horror by a deed which carried dread to the heart of every one — a deed more fiendish, more horrible than ever before perpetrated on this side of the snowy Sierra. Julia Bulette was found lying dead in her bed, foully murdered, and stiff and cold in her clotted gore. True, she was a woman of easy virtue. Yet hundreds in this city have had cause to bless her name for her many acts of charity. So much worse the crime. That woman probably had more real, warm friends in this community than any other; yet there was found at last a human being so fiendish and base as to crawl to her bedside in the dead hour of the night, and with violent hands, beat and strangle her to death — not for revenge, but in order to plunder her of these very articles of clothing and jewelry we see before us. What inhuman, unparalleled barbarity!"

Whether Millian was actually guilty or not is still being debated today, but the true outcome of the sensational murder, trial, and hanging was the phenomenal growth of Julia Bulette's legend.

In recent years it has been stated that she owned either a fancy gambling hall or an opulent bordello, that she was always attended by servants and rode through town in a coach-and-four, that she was one of the first women on the Comstock and the miners rallied to her defense during the Indian battles of 1860, and that she was not a white women but was a Louisiana Creole. All of these assertions are patently false.

In truth, the woman known as Julia Bulette was a Caucasian born in England in 1832. When very young she emigrated to New Orleans, there marrying a man named Smith. By 1852 she had appeared in California, working as a prostitute, and had adopted the pseudonym of Julia Bulette before moving to Virginia City in April, 1863.

On the Comstock she lived and worked simply as an upper-middle-class prostitute. The early-day volunteer firemen were her champions, calling her "Jule," and paid her a great tribute by naming her an honorary member of Engine Co. No. 1.

Never wealthy, she lived and worked alone in a small frame cottage at No. 4 North D Street, in the main red-light district. She could never have afforded servants or a coach, as when her estate was sold at auction after her death the proceeds amounting to less than $800 were insufficient to pay her outstanding debts. She did not even own the house she lived in.

Julia C. Bulette in the mid-1860's.

The extravagance of her legend is an outgrowth of the tourist boom which descended upon Virginia City in the early 1950's. The fence around her grave was moved to make it visible from C Street saloons, deeds of her selfless sacrifices for the miners were invented, an attractive but fictitious painting purported to be her was placed on display, totally erroneous books of her life story were published, a highly fictionalized episode about her was televised on "Bonanza," and even a local saloon was named in her honor.

In all truth, the *Territorial Enterprise* once described her as being "kind-hearted, liberal, benevolent, and charitable." While the facts of her life fall short of her legend, she must indeed have been a very exceptional woman for the time and place.

Eilley and Sandy Bowers: The Comstock's First Nabobs

Among the placer miners working the gravel of Gold Canyon in the early 1850's was Lemuel Sanford "Sandy" Bowers. A Missouri mule-skinner, Sandy had come to western Utah Territory as a driver for a small wagon train. It took but one look at gold mining for him to abandon his previous occupation, and he was soon busily sifting tons of earth through his rocker for a few dollars a day.

Another early settler was Mrs. Alex Cowan, who had come to western Utah's Carson County with her Mormon husband in 1855. Born Allison "Eilley" Orrum, she had emigrated from her native Scotland to the pioneer Mormon village of Nauvoo, Illinois. There she married Stephen Hunter, who brought her west to Salt Lake City, but she divorced him when he began to take additional wives. She and her second husband proceeded to purchase a ranch in Washoe Valley, then established a boardinghouse in Gold Canyon.

When Brigham Young recalled his far-flung colonists in 1857, Eilley's husband returned to Salt Lake alone. She obtained a second divorce, while continuing to operate the boardinghouse during summer months and live on the ranch in the winter. With the founding of Gold Hill in January, 1859, Eilley immediately built the second structure there, a combination log boardinghouse and restaurant.

One of her customers did not have the cash to settle his account, so Eilley accepted ten feet of a claim in Gold Hill. Another patron, Sandy Bowers, owned an adjoining ten feet. In August the two were married, which also united their holdings into a 20-foot mine known as the "Bowers claim."

The following year, with the discovery of the Comstock Lode prompting intensive development work, one of the richest surface ore deposits was found to lie on the Bowers' property. At its peak, when the mine was producing $100,000 a month, Eilley and Sandy Bowers found themselves rich beyond belief.

After years of poverty and unhappiness Eilley took great delight in spending their new-found wealth. Neither had received more than a rudimentary education, although Sandy had been a delegate to the futile 1859 convention which had attempted to create a separate territory in the Comstock region. Still they determined to hob-nob with the gentry, now that they were members of "high society."

A proper home was deemed necessary, and none but an opulent mansion would do. While it was under construction on Eilley's Washoe Valley ranch property, the Bowers traveled to Europe on a buying spree to obtain the furnishings it would require. They spent untold thousands on carpets, books, silver services, marble, and clothes, even collecting ivy from Westminster Abbey to transplant in Washoe Valley.

Eilley was childless, as her two natural children had died shortly after birth. When the mother of a day-old girl died on the voyage back to the U.S., the Bowers informally adopted the child. Named Margaret Persia, she accompanied them when they moved into the mansion that had cost $407,000.

Their life progressed like a fairy tale until Sandy died suddenly in 1868, leaving Eilley to again fend for herself. At the time of his death Sandy's estate was valued at only $638,000. He had sold stock in the mine for some reason, allowing control of the property to slip out of the Bowers' hands. An inept mine superintendent soon ran Eilley $30,000 in debt, so she decided a public raffle of all her property was the only way to raise sufficient funds. Forty thousand tickets were printed and offered for sale at $2.50 each. One thousand were given to Eilley and Persia, but many remained unsold when the raffle was held.

Fortunately Eilley won back her mansion, its furniture, and the 140 acres surrounding it. She immediately enlarged the building, adding bath houses to the pools, a dance pavilion, and picnic areas. In 1874 the place was opened to the public, quickly becoming a popular recreational area.

Another disaster occurred in July, though, when Persia also died suddenly at age 12. Eilley was grief-stricken, but creditors were again hammering at her door. In 1876 her property was sold at public auction to satisfy her debts, although she was permitted to live in a small cottage on the grounds. She attempted

This 19th century view of Bowers Mansion shows it decorated with an American flag, probably in celebration of a national holiday.

to burn the mansion one night, but only succeeded in destroying her own home, forcing her to move in with a friend in Virginia City.

Ever since coming to the area in the mid-1850's, Eilley had owned a crystal ball with which she claimed she could foretell the future. For a time she was able to eke out a small living this way, styling herself the "Washoe Seeress." She moved to Reno, then San Francisco, until she was finally placed in Oakland's Home of the King's Daughters where she died in 1903.

The mansion changed hands numerous times until it was purchased by the Reno Civic Women's Club and Washoe County in 1946. Today the grounds have been enlarged and the mansion restored to its 1860's appearance, providing summer recreation to thousands of persons annually.

The Bowers mine is another story altogether. It became part of William Sharon's Consolidated Imperial mine in 1876, although little ore was found below the 1600-foot level. In the late 1930's the Imperial was open-pitted by the Sutro Tunnel Coalition Company, which uncovered large quantities of low-grade ore within a few feet of Sandy Bowers' original claim. When Houston Oil & Minerals began working the Comstock in the late 1970's, it was on this same ground that they dug their enormous open pit mine to supply the new mill in American Flat. Of course, all traces of Sandy's mine are gone, but the "money to throw at the birds" which it provided enabled future generations to enjoy Bowers Mansion, one of the most attractive recreational parks in all of Nevada.

Miners' Unions

Early sketch of Comstock miners, c. 1860's. The cage on the extreme left of the 3-compartment shaft holds men ready to descend into the mine while the other two cages show men pushing, or "tramming," the one-ton ore cars used to remove waste rock or ore.

While giving a speech in 1911, Judge C. C. Goodwin stated that "California drew to her golden shores the pick of the world. Nevada drew to herself the pick of California." This was an inference that the 19th century Comstockers were superior people, a statement that none of the miners would have disputed. They received the highest wages paid any laborers. To insure their financial status the first Miners' Protective Association was organized in Virginia City on May 30, 1863, with the Gold Hill miners soon following suit. The purpose of the organization, as stipulated in its constitution and by-laws, was "the practice of those virtues which elevate and adorn society and remind man of his duty to his fellow-man; the elevation of the position, and maintenance of the rights of the miner."

The initial success in organizing such a union was tempered during the slack period of 1865-66, when many miners had to take a reduction in wages just to keep their jobs. The miners reorganized when production began to increase in 1867, finding little opposition to their demands. However, one recalcitrant mine foreman was tied to a hoist cable until he acquiesced to the $4 per day minimum, while another superintendent had to be hidden by Father Manogue after his proposal to cut wages had turned a group of miners into a vengeance-seeking mob.

One shrewd move by Adolph Sutro, while he was attempting to secure financing to begin excavating the Sutro Tunnel, was to portray the proposed project as a means of ventilating the underground mines, draining excess water, and providing an escape route in the event of a fire or cave-in. Working conditions were bad enough in the Comstock mines, but when Sutro began circulating engravings showing a "rich mine owner driving six fast horses and contemptuously covering a worn-out miner with dust," the support of the Miners' Union was assured. They purchased an interest in the Sutro Tunnel Company for $50,000, which helped to begin work on the tunnel.

As the mines progressed deeper, working conditions suffered a dramatic deterioration. The Miners' Union tried to compensate for this by proposing an eight-hour shift as early as 1867, but this did not become a reality until 1872. Mine owner John P. Jones, who was then a candidate for the U.S. Senate, ordered this shift reduction of all underground miners in the Crown Point mine. William Sharon, the opposing candidate, quickly ordered the same shift reduction in all the Comstock mines he controlled to keep the miners' vote from swinging to Jones. However, as the idea had originated with Jones, it was perhaps instrumental in his big victory over Sharon.

Another object of the union was to keep Chinese labor out of the mines. No mine superintendent had dared to hire any Chinese during the 1860's, but the V&T RR used a great number of them to grade the roadbed during the railroad's construction. Even this isolated case of Chinese employment was impossible for the miners to bear, so on September 29, 1869, some 350 men marched upon the Orientals then working on the roadbed near the Overman mine. The County Sheriff read an order to the miners to disperse, then read them the riot act when he was answered with laughter. By this time the Chinese laborers were racing off through the sagebrush, so the miners calmly marched back to Gold Hill and Virginia City to the accompaniment of fifes and drums. Eight days later William Sharon's pleas induced the union to allow the Chinese to complete their work on the railroad, but they were never again employed *en masse* on any other Comstock project.

The Miners' Union was also created as a benevolent institution. Dues of $2 per month were automatically deducted from each member's pay, which went into a general fund. A sick or disabled miner was aided financially until he could return to work. The family of a miner killed in any way was also assisted as well as possible, and it was customery for each member to donate a day's pay to the family of such a deceased miner.

The union provided a recreational outlet as well. When the fire of 1875 destroyed the Miners' Union Hall, another was immediately erected on B Street. It contained an assembly hall, ballroom, chess room, and a public library. Union members had access to the 2,200 books free of charge, while non-members were required to pay a fee of 50¢ per month.

When Comstock mine production reached its peak in the mid-1870's, one final demonstration took

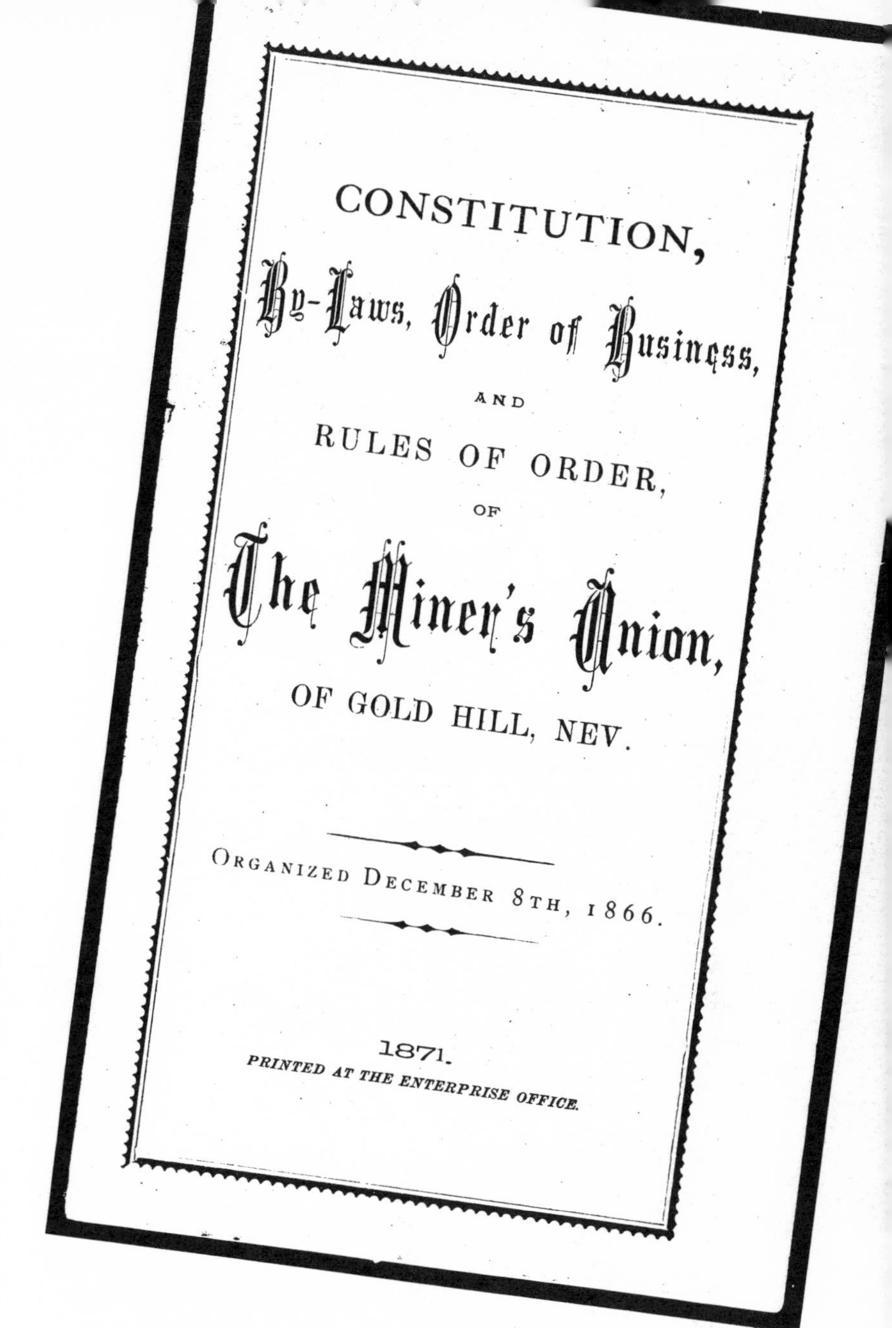
CONSTITUTION,
By-Laws, Order of Business,
AND
RULES OF ORDER,
OF
The Miner's Union,
OF GOLD HILL, NEV.

ORGANIZED DECEMBER 8TH, 1866.

1871.
PRINTED AT THE ENTERPRISE OFFICE.

place. Fifty-eight men were employed at the Imperial mine in 1877 who were earning less than the union demanded. Thousands of union members quietly marched to the mine, insisting that all men working for reduced wages be fired. The superintendent quickly ordered the men out of the mine, meekly submitting to the immense power the union had over the mine owners and foremen.

With the decline of the Comstock, the local unions also faded away. But they had most assuredly left their mark. Members of the Virginia City union helped organize similar institutions in California, including the ones at Grass Valley and Sutter Creek. This latter organization prompted a bloody collision known as the Amador War, while in Nevada the Goldfield Miners' Union had their own bitter labor-management confrontation in the winter of 1907-08. Today much of the benefits and improved working conditions which miners through the West enjoy are a direct result of the pioneer movement in Virginia City.

The early one-man operation in Gold Hill utilized a hand-cranked windlass to raise an ore bucket rather than a motorized hoist (left). Miners pause on a drift switch at the 2700-foot level of the Monte Cristo mine. Each man carries a pointed iron candleholder which is driven into nearby timbering to provide light. At lower right is the facade of the Virginia City Miners Union Hall building.

RULES OF ORDER.

During the continuance of the meeting, silence must be observed—the officers and members retaining their respective seats—and no one leaving the room without the permission of the President or Vice President.

No member shall, by conversation or otherwise, interrupt the business of the Union, or refuse to obey the Chair.

The President while presiding, will state every question coming before the Union, and immediately before putting it to vote shall ask: "Are you ready for the question?" Should no member rise to speak, or by silence indicate their readiness, he shall rise to take the question; and after he has risen, no member shall be permitted to speak upon it. He shall pronounce the result or decision of the Union upon all subjects.

Every member, when he speaks, or offers a motion, shall rise, and respectfully address the presiding officer. While speaking, he shall confine himself to the question under debate, avoiding all personality and indecorous language, as well as any reflection upon the Union or its members.

Should two or more members rise to speak at the same time, the Chair shall decide who is entitled to the floor.

No member shall disturb another in his speech, unless to call him to order for words spoken.

If a member, while speaking, shall be called to order, at the request of the Chair he shall cease speaking and take his seat until the question of order is determined, when, if permitted, he may again proceed.

No member shall speak more than once on the same question until all the members wishing to speak shall have had an opportunity to do so, nor more than twice without permission of the Chair.

When any communication petition, or memorial is presented, before it is read a brief statement of its contents shall be made by the introducer to the Chair.

No motion shall be subject to action unless seconded and stated by the Chair.

Any member may call for a division of a question when the sense will admit of it.

When a question is before the Union, no motion shall be received, unless to close, the previous question, to lay on the table, to postpone indefinitely, to postpone to a certain time, to refer, to amend, and shall have precedence in the order herein arranged, the three first of which shall be decided without debate.

After any question, except one of indefinite postponement, has been decided, any two members who voted in the majority may, at the same meeting, move for a reconsideration thereof.

Members present can vote on any question before the Union, provided they are in good standing.

No amendment shall be received except it be in writing.

All questions not provided for by the Constitution, By-Laws, Rules of Order, or by the general laws of the Union, shall be determined by a majority of the members at a regular meeting.

These rules may be suspended for a special purpose by a vote of two thirds of the members present.

Volunteer Fire Companies

During the first year following the discovery of the Comstock Lode, the population of the "Washoe Mining Region" jumped from less than 200 to nearly 3,000. In the ensuing mad scramble little thought was given to permanent structures. Many a miner's home was no more than a tent or dugout, while the better buildings were constructed of whatever wood could be freighted in. As a consequence, the danger of fire was a constant worry, particularly in Virginia City where high winds and a scarcity of water meant that a small blaze could easily destroy the town.

In the fall of 1860 the first volunteer fire organization was formed when a group of local residents met at the International hotel. Their only equipment consisted of pails, which were to be used as a bucket brigade in the event of a fire.

The first true fire company was organized on March 4, 1861, with the creation of Virginia Engine Company No. 1. The membership roster soon boasted 65 men, their equipment consisting of one of the west's most powerful horse-drawn engines. At nearly the same time the Nevada Hook & Ladder Co. No. 1 was formed to compliment the first organization. The 65 men in its ranks usually worked in tandem with the engine company whenever they were called out.

By late 1863 the two pioneer companies had been joined by three others — the Young America Engine Co. No. 2, Eagle Engine Co. No. 3, and Washoe Engine Co. No. 4 — while the Hook & Ladder Co. of Gold Hill had also been formed. Unfortunately, the cooperation between companies which had originally existed soon dissolved into fierce competition and rivalry.

Virginia City's first serious fire occurred on August

With houses in such congestion, it is little wonder that fires would spread quickly (left). While Father Manogue rendered aid during the Yellow Jacket mine fire of 1869, the men of the Liberty Volunteer Hose Co. No. 1 of Gold Hill were among those who responded to fight the blaze (below).

29, 1863, when a blaze broke out in a carpenter's shop in the rear of Patrick Lynch's saloon. The volunteer firemen responded, but a fight immediately broke out between Engine Co. No. 2 on the one side, and the men of both Engine Co. No. 1 and the Hook & Ladder No. 1 on the other. Bricks were hurled back and forth, felling a number of participants, but the only fatality resulted when John Cullen shot and killed a fireman named Richardson. While the fight diverted the firemen's attention, the blaze spread rapidly. By the time it was extinguished the main business district between Sutton and Taylor Streets and from A to B Street was leveled.

As Cullen was a member of Engine Co. No. 2, the opposing firemen swore vengeance. They quickly surrounded No. 2's fire house and threatened to tear it apart. However, the men of Engine Co. No. 2 were barricaded inside at the time with a small cannon loaded with grapeshot, and its presence finally caused the attackers to wisely withdraw. This was the only serious battle between rival fire companies, but the feuds continued for many years thereafter.

In another sense, the Comstock was fortunate to have such a rough and ready group of men in their midst. A contemporary historian wrote, "That class of men who were made to move the world, delight in

the excitement and exertion incident to the service in a fire company." Many of them had served in fire companies back east, particulary in New York, and were thus firmly devoted to the Union side in the Civil War. During the early 1860's, when pro-Confederate sentiments were punishable by carrying a heavy sandbag around the parade ground at Fort Churchill, the firemen often meted out swifter retribution by simply beating an offender senseless. This pro-Northern determination of the red-shirted fire "boys" was perhaps one of the dominant reasons why the Comstock remained so firmly on the Union side.

Many stories are told of the turbulent and often violent lives of prominent firemen. Tom Peasley, who organized both the Engine Co. No. 1 and Hook & Ladder No. 1, was perhaps the best known of them all. Fearless and hard-driving, he whipped the two original fire companies into shape while also becoming the unofficial leader of the pro-Union movement among the men. He met an untimely death in 1866 when he was murdered by Martin Barnhart in Car-

The hand pumper of the Young America Engine Company below saw action in many local fires, such as the one at right. On the opposite page, a visiting San Francisco fireman was photographed in Virginia City.

son City's Ormsby House hotel, but Mark Twain immortalized him by patterning his famous "Buck Fanshaw" character after Peasley.

By the mid-1870's, Virginia City had also seen the formation of Knickerbocker Engine Co. No. 5, Confidence (later called Monumental) Engine Co. No. 6, and the Hand-in-Hand Hose Co. No. 1. Yet when the great fire of October, 1875 broke out, even this large number of firemen was unable to stop the disaster. When it was over, all of the fire equipment except that of the Monumental and Young America companies had been destroyed by the flames, and most of the fire houses were among the 1,300 buildings burned.

As the Comstock was in a bonanza period at the time, Virginia City was quick to start rebuilding. However, the days of the volunteer firemen were past. A paid fire department was authorized by the legislature to take their place, and new fire equipment was ordered. With the successful completion of the Comstock's new water supply system, additional mains and fire hydrants did away with the old man-powered pumpers.

Today Virginia City is again served by an efficient volunteer fire department equipped with modern fire-fighting apparatus, while Silver City has its own separate department, yet the memory of those pioneer firemen is very much alive. A fire museum on C Street is open during the summer, but most important is the annual Firemen's Muster held every August. More than 200 units meet in Virginia City to compete with such equipment as hand pumpers, hose carts, and bucket brigades. Often in period costume, the men of these companies recreate the rivalry and vibrance of the red-shirted volunteers who were so much a part of the Comstock's early days.

The Sutro Tunnel

Adolph Heinrich Joseph Sutro was a brilliant man who lived to see the successful completion of practically every project he ever attempted, including the building of the greatest construction project ever devised on the Comstock Lode — the Sutro Tunnel. Born in Prussia on April 29, 1830, Sutro was reared in the family's business of manufacturing woolen cloth. He was an accomplished engineer by the time he set sail for New York in 1850 with his mother and nine brothers and sisters.

Posters and advertisements proclaiming the wonders of California were everywhere in New York, prompting Sutro to book passage for himself and a load of trade goods less than two weeks after he had arrived in America. He sold his wares immediately upon landing in San Francisco, then he went into the commission business where he bought and sold goods for others. By April, 1851, he was in partnership with his cousin in a small dry goods store in Stockton.

Drainpipe of the Sutro Tunnel.

Soon he was operating two stores in San Francisco, then he added a tobacco stand and real estate to his holdings. Financially well-off, he married and had the first of his many children before joining the ill-fated rush to Fraser River in 1858. He returned disappointed and without having made a cent, so when news of the Comstock discovery electrified California the following year, he was naturally hesitant about participating in another fiasco. However, Sutro did make a brief trip to Virginia City in the spring of 1860 to look the place over. Upon his return he published a report in a California newspaper which proposed, among other things, the building of a railroad from the Comstock to the Carson River and a deep tunnel to the base of the lode for ventilation, drainage, and access to ore.

By May he was back on the Comstock for another visit, this time to acquire ore samples. He was certain that there must be a more effective way to recover the gold and silver it contained, so when he again returned to San Francisco he devoted his time to experimenting with this problem. By April, 1861, a new process had been found, prompting Sutro to sell all of his California businesses to build an 8-stamp mill at Dayton. A contract to work Gould & Curry ore soon came his way, and by 1863 he was making a profit of $10,000 monthly.

The idea of a long tunnel to intersect the deep mines had become an obsession by this time. When his Dayton mill mysteriously burned in late 1863, Sutro's insurance money enabled him to retire from the business world. He concentrated on promoting the idea of his tunnel, even hiring George Ernst to make the first surveys of its proposed location. A lobbying effort in the first Nevada State Legislature produced a franchise in 1865, thus granting him permission to dig the tunnel. Nothing more was needed but financing, and Sutro was optimistic that digging could begin within a year.

The Sutro Tunnel Company was organized with Senator Stewart as its president, then Sutro set out to inform the world what a success the project would be. Baron Richthofen was hired to write a glowing report, thousands of copies of which were printed

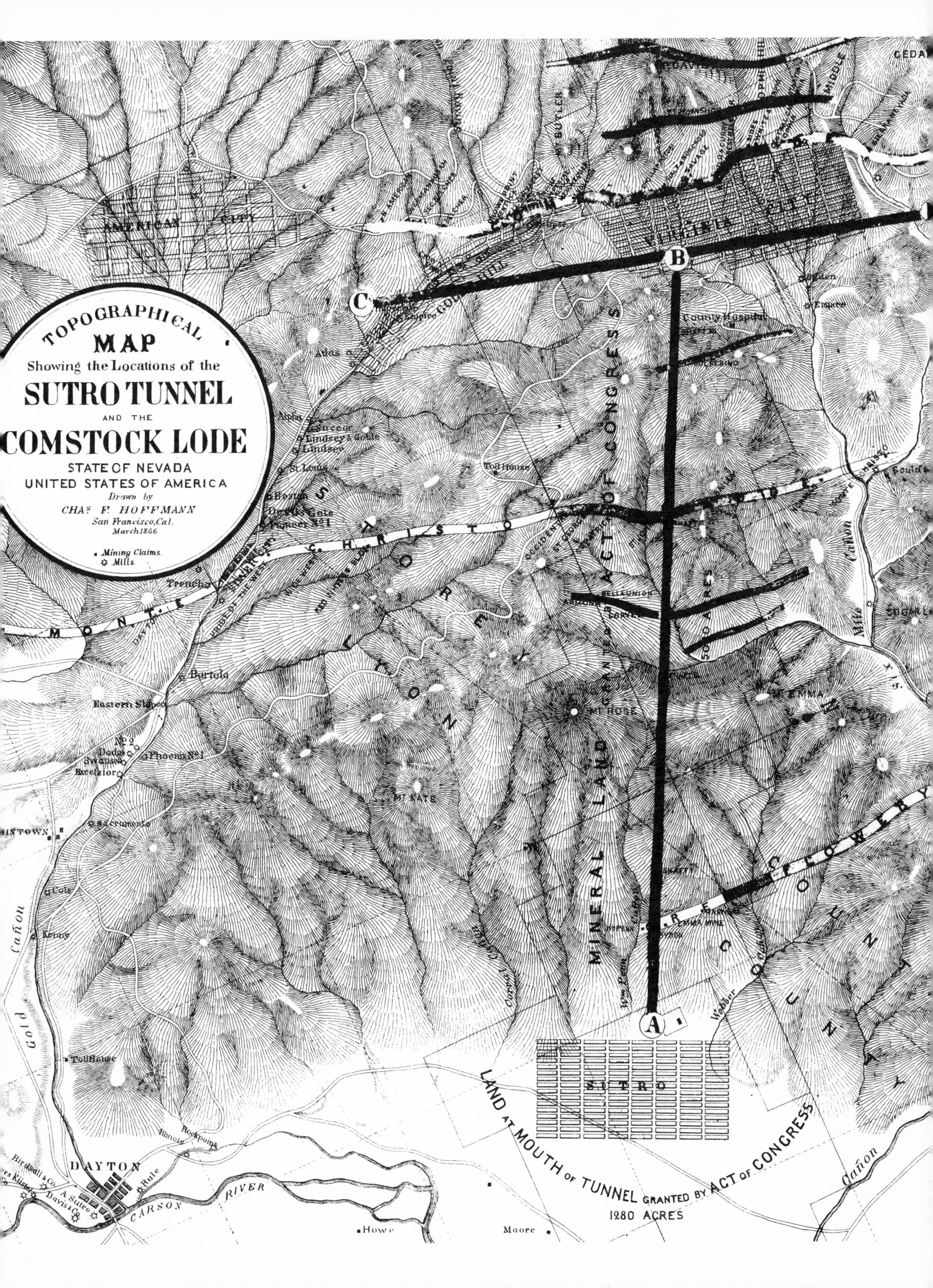
TOPOGRAPHICAL
MAP
Showing the Locations of the
SUTRO TUNNEL
AND THE
COMSTOCK LODE
STATE OF NEVADA
UNITED STATES OF AMERICA
Drawn by
CHAS F. HOFFMANN
San Francisco, Cal.
March 1866
Mining Claims.
Mills.
AMERICAN CITY
VIRGINIA CITY
GOLD HILL
County Hospital
Toll House
MONTE CHRISTO
MINERAL LAND GRANTED BY ACT OF CONGRESS
LYON
MT ROSE
MT KATE
SUTRO
LAND AT MOUTH OF TUNNEL GRANTED BY ACT OF CONGRESS
1280 ACRES
DAYTON
CARSON RIVER
Gold Cañon
Eastern Slope
Bartola
Trench
Sacramento
Cole
Kenny
Toll House
Rock point
Illinois
Rule
Howe
Moore
Empire
Alpha
St. Louis
Atlas
Phoenix No 1
Excelsior
Swansea
Dodge
No 2
Cañon
A
B
C

Adolph Sutro is in his usual pose. More than twenty significant documents were published during the eight years Sutro fought to build his tunnel. Both sides levied extravagant charges, but Sutro eventually prevailed. The opulent Victorian mansion (far right) built by Sutro at the town of Sutro. Abandoned and in disrepair, it was destroyed by fire in 1941.

and circulated by Sutro in 1866. The Bank of California also favored the idea, so Sutro set off to visit financiers in the east with letters of reference from both Sharon and Ralston.

The land title still had be be affirmed, but Congress quickly passed the "Sutro Tunnel Act" on July 25, 1866, which not only granted him the land but also stated that mining companies using the services of the tunnel must pay royalties. Thus armed, he began the rounds of financial backers and institutions in New York but found every one of them reluctant to invest.

Undaunted, Sutro began a tireless publicity campaign but he continued to run into stiff opposition. The Bank of California had begun to plan for their proposed railroad to transport ore, rather than use Sutro's idea of a gravity system within his tunnel. They also had decided such a major enterprise should not be allowed to exist unless they controlled it, as they did so much of the business on the Lode. Sharon and Ralston knew they could never control Sutro, so they withdrew all support, then they informed other financial institutions throughout the

THE STYLE OF WARFARE
AS CARRIED ON BY THE
CALIFORNIA BANK RING.

OUTRAGEOUS ATTACKS ON THE HONOR AND INTEGRITY OF MR. SUTRO.

WHAT MONEY WILL DO!

The California Bank ring have r
cry of "Stop thief!" whenever th
an iniquity, and it is significant t
papers which they hired for the p
denly "chopped" round.

Below will be found some e
News, a paper published at G
Lode, which articles appeared
the war of the Bank of Califo
nel first openly commenced:

[The *Even*

"THE SUTRO TUNNEL.—We are p
ing adopted encouraging this measu
result in *incalculable benefit to this se*
"The Sutro Tunnel enterprise is
...the aid of the National Go

DEAR SI
the law gra
to the Sutro
of the legisla

THE COMSTOCK COMPANIE

DEFY THE EXECUTION OF A LAW OF CONGRESS.

Extracts from the Records on file in the General Land O
certified to by the Commissioner.

From the following extracts made from records on
in the General Land Office, concerning applications
patents on the Comstock Lode, and protests filed by di
ent parties, it appears—

1st. That the owners of the mines on the Comst

world that they would not look favorably on anyone else who supported it.

Travels to New York, Washington, and all across Europe proved fruitless in his quest for funds. Then the disastrous fire in the Yellow Jacket mine occurred in 1869, causing 37 men to die. Sutro immediately began explaining to the Miners' Union how his tunnel could have provided an escape route for the men and how proper ventilation would lower the chances of future fires. They backed him solidly, even subscribing $50,000 to the Sutro Tunnel Company, and this gave the project its first real support on the Comstock. The first shovelful of dirt was finally turned on October 19, 1869, marking the beginning of tunnel construction.

Raising money was still a challenge as the Bank of California remained firmly against the project, but in 1871 Sutro finally found investors in England and Germany. It was an uphill fight all the way but on July 8, 1878, the Sutro Tunnel connected with the 1,640-foot level of the Savage mine. It had taken more than eight years to dig, since the tunnel was an astounding 3.8 miles long.

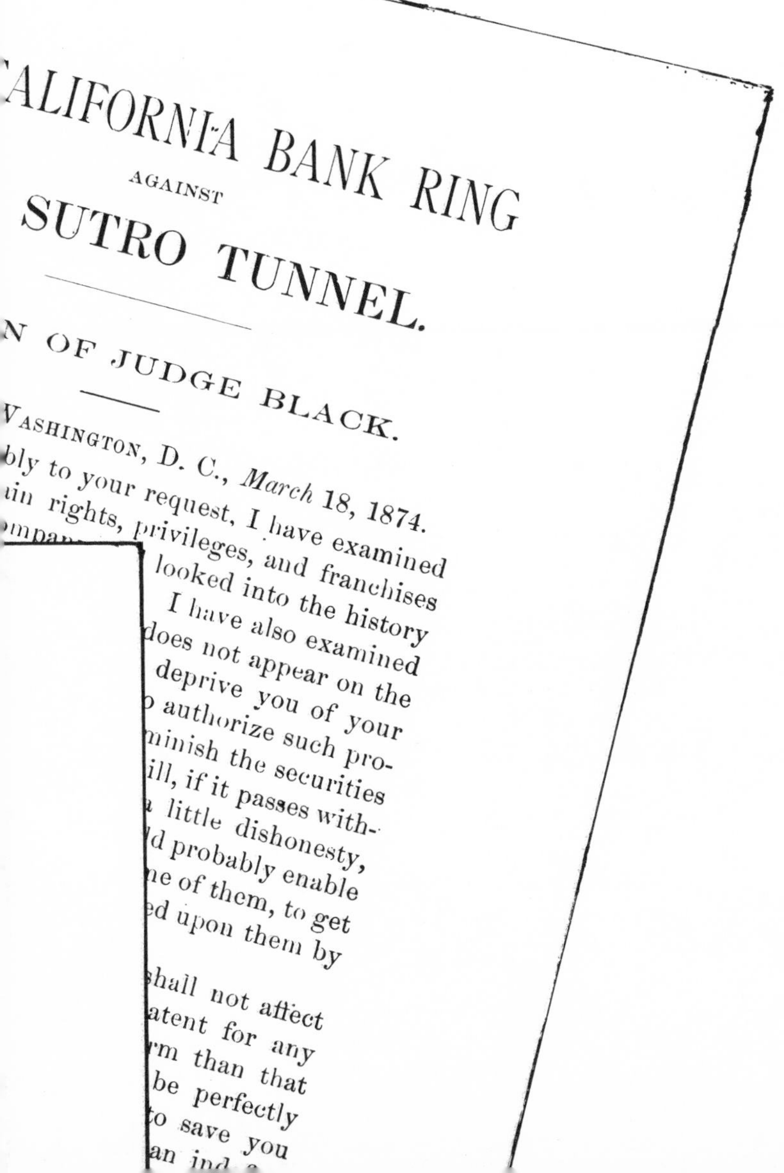

ALIFORNIA BANK RING

AGAINST

SUTRO TUNNEL.

N OF JUDGE BLACK.

VASHINGTON, D. C., *March* 18, 1874.

bly to your request, I have examined
ain rights, privileges, and franchises
looked into the history
I have also examined
does not appear on the
deprive you of your
authorize such pro-
minish the securities
ill, if it passes with-
little dishonesty,
d probably enable
ne of them, to get
ed upon them by

hall not affect
atent for any
rm than that
be perfectly
o save you
an ind

Sutro had built his own town, appropriately named Sutro, at the mouth of the tunnel three miles east of Dayton. Here he built a mansion, planted trees along the streets and even founded a newspaper called the *Independent*. By the time the tunnel was completed, though, the Comstock mines had already been extended far deeper than the 1,600-foot level where it intersected. With the expense the mines had already incurred in building huge engines and hoisting works, and with the contracts the V&T RR already had for transporting ore, the gravity system proposed to move ore down the tunnel was not used. The tunnel's only real value was in providing an egress for the huge quantities of hot water found in the underground workings and in ventilation. Thus Sutro's little town never became the milling center he had envisioned, but instead it soon withered away to nothing.

Sutro sold his stock in the tunnel in 1880, receiving a little less than $1 million for his five-twelfth ownership of the company. The tunnel had been completed, for which he had worked and dreamed for so long, but the business of running it was not for him. He quit Nevada forever, moving to a mansion in San Francisco.

Later in life Sutro invested heavily in California real estate. He also purchased 1½ miles of Pacific shoreline where he built the Sutro Baths, converted the Cliff House into a respectable family resort, and built his magnificent Sutro Heights. His library was said to hold 125,000 books, including 15% of all surviving volumes published between 1455 and 1500. He even served as San Francisco's mayor, although an ineffectual one, from 1895 to 1897.

Adolph Sutro died on August 8, 1898. Only 68 years old, he had nevertheless lived an intensely energetic life. His projects were legion, and many were of extreme beauty and grandeur, but the one hardest fought and perhaps longest remembered was that of the Sutro Tunnel.

Virginia & Truckee Railroad

It is a paradox in Nevada that wherever rich deposits of gold and silver were found, water was usually in short supply. Such was certainly the case on the Comstock, so many of the giant quartz reduction mills needed to refine the ore were of necessity located along the banks of the Carson River, seven miles or more south of Virginia City. It soon became evident, though, that the cost of freighting huge quantities of ore to the 31 mills in the area was becoming prohibitive, as was the price teamsters charged to haul firewood back up the mountain to the Comstock to feed the boilers needed in working the ever-deepening mines. The Bank of California, which had acquired most of the major mines during the 1860's, quickly realized that this shipping problem was taking increasingly larger bites out of their profits. A permanent solution was needed, so William Sharon and his bank decided to build a railroad.

Several previous attempts to build a railroad out of Virginia City had all failed. Two different lines were promoted as early as 1861, before the first Virginia & Truckee RR was approved by a special act of the Territorial Legislature on December 20, 1862. The legislature decreed only that it must pass through Carson City on its way to the Truckee River, but insufficient capital stopped the project. It was not until the Bank of California undertook to build the road seven years later that the project finally became a reality.

Ground was broken on February 18, 1869, but delays in the arrival of equipment postponed the laying of the first rails until September 28. Once begun, construction proceeded quickly until Virginia City and Carson City were connected by rail on November 12. As the transcontinental railroad passed along the Truckee River only 30 miles to the north, it was decided that the grandest of all mining

The Tahoe *and another V&T engine with their crews (above). A snowplow-equipped locomotive kicks up a spray of snow on the track entering Virginia City.*

towns should be connected to it. On August 24, 1872, the line from Carson to the four-year-old community of Reno was completed, directly connecting Virginia City with San Francisco and the east coast.

The trestles, tunnels, and tortuous curves necessary to navigate down the steep mountainsides made the V&T an expensive line to construct. In September, 1873, a published table of costs showed that the amount expended to build the line and purchase equipment equalled $52,107 for every mile of track between Virginia City and Reno. The transportation problem had been solved, though, for by the following year 36 trains per day were being run on the track between Carson and Virginia alone.

Only the best in equipment and rolling stock were purchased for the V&T. The original rails were rolled in Sheffield, England; the first 16 of the lines's 29 locomotives were the best that could be turned out in the famous shops of Booth, Baldwin, American, and Cooke; and its coaches were splendid examples of plush Victorian rail transportation. So many gold and silver ingots were shipped via the V&T, either to the U.S. Mint at Carson City or to banking firms in San Francisco, that a special car had to be constructed just for this cargo. Even its passengers were noteworthy. Besides the frequent excursion and picnic trains to Bowers' Mansion or Steamboat, which delighted Comstock miners and their families, the V&T also carried Baron Rothschild; Presidents Grant, Hayes, Hoover, and Theodore Roosevelt; plus dozens of governors, senators, and foreign realty.

So much revenue was generated by the V&T during the bonanza years of the early 1870's that the three Bank of California directors who actually owned the railroad — William Sharon, William Ralston, and Darius O. Mills — were sharing profits of $100,000 per month. However, as the mine production diminished in the latter years of the 19th century, so did the fortunes of the railroad. Mills, who had succeeded or outlived his partners, tried unsuccessfully to sell the line to the Southern Pacific RR in 1900.

By 1905 the line was foundering, so an attempt was made to generate additional income by extending track south from Carson to the agricultural town of Minden. Farm produce largely replaced silver bullion on freight way-bills, but the new business was sufficient to keep the V&T running. However, diminished passenger travel and increasing operating expenses prompted the V&T's purchase of three motor railcars, which were intermittently used in lieu of the costly steam engines to haul both passengers and baggage through the early 1940's.

Lack of traffic and high maintenance costs finally caused the abandonment and removal of the tracks between Carson and Virginia City in 1938. The line from Minden to Reno saw increased business during World War II, when gas rationing reduced highway travel, but the reprieve was brief. In 1950, after 80 years of operation, engine number 27 pulled the last train into Reno, and the Virginia & Truckee Railroad ceased to exist.

But legends die hard, especially in Nevada. In 1976 a shortened reconstruction of the line was opened to the public in Virginia City, returning the sound of live-steam locomotives to the Comstock once again. Although passengers can ride the modern track only from Washington Street to the first tunnel, plans are underway to extend it along the original roadbed at least down to Gold Hill.

Since the life of the V&T had extended well into the 20th century, much of its equipment has been preserved. The sight of four of the original locomotives are probably very familiar to most people, as they were used extensively by Hollywood studios in the making of television shows and motion pictures. Besides some of the old cars undergoing restoration at the new V&T car-barn in Virginia City, a state-owned railroad museum in Carson City is skillfully refurbishing their collection of 1870's V&T engines and coaches, while a new railroad museum in Sacramento has magnificently rebuilt three original locomotives.

Today the whistle of a V&T engine signalling for a crossing still echoes down Six-Mile Canyon, while its century-old predecessors have become gleaming museum pieces. They are both reminders of the glory years when this line was truthfully known as "the richest short line railroad in the world."

Passengers wend their way among deep drifts at the Virginia City depot.

CANN

V&T engine number 4, the "Virginia," pulls an ore train on the southeast edge of Virginia City. This rare view was taken in the 1890's, during one of the last periods of Comstock mine production, and shows ore probably destined for one of the Carson River mills.

Cousin Jacks and Tommyknockers

As in every western mining rush, there were always more men looking for work than there were jobs during the early years of the Comstock. Naturally, as the mines were driven inexorably deeper, men with experience in hard-rock mining were given preference over all others. An 1880 census listing the 28 nationalities of the 2,770 miners then employed on the Comstock showed that 816 were Irish, 770 were American, and a surprising 640 were from England. It is safe to assume at this late date that a majority of them were from Cornwall, site of some of the world's oldest underground mines.

The products of the Cornish tin and copper mines had been sought after in the days of ancient Greece, but by the early 19th century Cornishmen were feeling the pinch of tough times that were occurring throughout Great Britain. The Highland Clearances were driving great numbers of Scots to America, the potato famine was forcing thousands of Irishmen from their homeland, and so were the men of Cornwall leaving England for new mineral areas. They quickly found work in California and Colorado, but nowhere was their knowledge of deep mining more in demand than on the Comstock Lode.

The nickname "Cousin Jack" was soon applied to all men from Cornwall. It seemed that as quickly as a Cornishman was hired to work in a mine, he would immediately begin to plead for a job for his "cousin, Jack," who was anxiously waiting for word of employment. The nickname spread far and wide, for even today Cornishmen still living in England are aware of the appellation.

Besides bringing their skills and strong backs to the Comstock, Cornishmen also brought the Tommyknocker, their brand of leprechaun. Known as *bucca* in the language of Cornwall, these tiny imps lived deep in the stopes and adits of hard-rock mines. They were both troublesome and protective, but could cause a miner to have the very worst luck if he did not provide for them.

Some miners believed that the Tommyknockers would make their tapping sounds to indicate where rich ore lay. Others feared the knocks, claiming that they were the spirits of men who had died trying to pick their way out of a rock-fall. However, most miners believed that while the Tommyknockers were mischevious, they would always use their knocks to warn men of a coming disaster, thus giving them time to escape.

When no danger threatened, the little people delighted in playing pranks on the miners. If a candle blew out at an inopportune time, or a small piece of rock fell from the roof of the mine to bounce off a man's head, or a tool which was positively left in a particular place turned up missing, then the event was always explained as just another Tommyknocker trick. Pity the poor man who did not believe in them, though, or refused to leave a bit of his dinner pastie for them. Bad luck, or worse, was certain to be headed his way very soon!

The supremacy of Cornishmen over other miners created much jealousy, made worse when some mine owners began paying higher wages to Cousin Jacks than to men of any other nationality. Miners' Unions were particularly outraged at this practice, as typified by the one in Cherry Creek. Located in eastern Nevada's White Pine County, this union was founded in 1879 specifically to combat this custom.

The Cousin Jacks perservered, however, enriching Nevada with both their knowledge and their lore. Descendants of the original miners are still to be found scattered throughout the state, but it is the Tommyknockers who have truly grown and prospered. Cornishman or not, there is hardly a miner working underground in Nevada today who does not believe in the little people. Some diehards refuse to admit their existence, but they will then usually shrug and state "it's bad luck to talk about them." Pasties are now eaten only as a treat, but a scrap from a miner's lunchbox is usually left behind when the midday meal is eaten — and a weather ear is always alert for the danger signal of a tiny tapping sound.

This giant Cornish pump, used in the Union mine in Virginia City, was the last of its kind to be installed on the Comstock.

Recipe For a Cornish Pastie

Along with the impish Tommyknockers, Cornishmen also brought their own brand of cooking to the Comstock. Known as a pastie (to rhyme with nasty, not tasty), this wholesome meat pie was taken hot from the oven, wrapped in sheets of any sort of handy paper, and placed in the miner's lunchpail. By dinnertime it was still warm, providing a hearty meal deep in the mines.

Pasties quickly became a Virginia City favorite, and are still served there on special occasions. This recipe was brought to the Comstock from Cornwall by Katie Kick, who is today the only true Cousin Jack remaining in Virginia City. It is guaranteed to be the same as that used more than a century ago:

Take 8 oz. flour, 3 oz. lard, ½ teasp. salt, and a little *cold* water. Mix together quickly; do not overhandle. Divide pastry into 3 parts and refrigerate.

Mix together ½ lb. top round steak cut into small pieces, 3 peeled and chipped medium potatoes, 1 peeled and cut up medium onion, 1 scraped and chipped carrot, and 1 peeled and chipped small rutabaga.

Preheat oven to 350°. Roll out the 3 parts of pastry to about the size of an average plate. On ½ of each of the three circles place ⅓ of the filling, salt and pepper to taste, and dot with butter. Fold over top half of the circle, sealing firmly. Make small hole in the top for steam and brush with beaten egg. Place 3 pasties on a floured cookie sheet, pushing close together so they are high. Bake 10 minutes at 350°, then reduce heat to 300° for 90 minutes. Makes 3 medium or 2 large.

The Bonanza Firm: Mackay, Fair, Flood and O'Brien

While tales of his generosity are common, making him by far the most well-known of the "Big Bonanza" kings, John Mackay's early life is little known. Born on November 28, 1831 in Dublin, Ireland, Mackay accompanied his family to New York when he was nine. There his father died two years later, forcing the youth to abandon school to provide for his mother and sister. Some biographers claim that he worked as a shoe-shine boy while others state he clerked in a grocery store, but it is known that at the age of 16 he was apprenticed to William Webb's shipyard. His work on the construction of side-wheel steamers developed his natural talent with tools, which he would later put to good use on the Comstock Lode.

In 1851, the 20-year-old Mackay sailed to California, where he spent the next eight years ekeing out a bare existence as a placer miner near Downieville. When news of the Washoe silver discovery was trumpeted on the Mother Lode in late 1859, he decided to try his luck over the mountains in Utah Territory. As soon as the passes were open in the spring of 1860, he and his partner Jack O'Brien walked to the ragged little community which had just been named Virginia City.

An often-repeated Comstock legend tells of Mackay and O'Brien's entry into camp. As they topped the last rise, and could see the wooden shacks of Virginia City ahead, O'Brien is said to have paused, turned to his friend and asked, "Have you any money?" When Mackay replied that he hadn't a cent, O'Brien then pulled his last half dollar from his pocket. As he tossed it out into the sagebrush he said, "Now we'll walk into the camp like gentlemen." In later years Mackay never disputed the story but only stated, "That's what Jack did with his money all his life."

Mackay was first employed on the Comstock as a common miner, earning $4 a day. He soon graduated to timberman, which paid $6, then in 1861 he quit working for others when he set himself up as an independent mining contractor. His first commission was to run a cross-cut for the Union mine, a job he accomplished so well that others were quick to hire him.

By 1863, after acquiring part ownership of four small mines, he entered into a partnership with J. M. Walker to manage the Bullion mine. Though it proved to be a failure, the experience taught the two men enough to purchase control of the Kentuck mine when it became available during the depression of 1865. The following year the mine hit a rich orebody, whereupon Walker sold out to Mackay for $600,000. With large profits from the Kentuck mine rolling in, Mackay married Marie Bryant and built a small frame house on the corner of Taylor and Howard Streets in Virginia City.

Two years later he entered into the decisive agreement with James Fair, James Flood, and William O'Brien to wrest control of the Hale & Norcross mine from William Sharon. Mackay's share in the enterprise was 37.5 percent, Fair's was 25 percent, while Flood and O'Brien each had 18.75 percent. This division of interests remained unchanged throughout the entire period which the "Bonanza Firm" operated together.

A fairly good discovery in the Hale & Norcross in 1869 brought even more wealth to Mackay's coffers. After the birth of his son, John Jr., in 1870, he decided to take his family on a tour of Europe. Mrs. Mackay became so enamoured of Paris life that she never came back to Virginia City, but did return to San Francisco to set up a Nob Hill household.

Mackay, meanwhile, was far too busy to be concerned with his society-seeking wife. He and his partners began acquiring shares of the Consolidated Virginia mine, and by the time of the stockholders meeting of January 11, 1872, they had gained control. It was on the 1,200-foot level of this mine that the "Big Bonanza" was discovered in March, 1873.

A year later his son Clarence was born in San Francisco, following which Mrs. Mackay happily set up a well-endowed permanent home in Paris. Wealthy beyond expectations, and free of the burdens of a family, Mackay immersed himself in his mining ventures. In 1875 the Bonanza Firm opened the Nevada Bank of San Francisco to compete with the Bank of California on the Comstock. He also devoted much time to the running of their many mines, mills, and other ventures, but the returns began to diminish as production of the great Comstock mines tapered off in the late 1870's. Realizing that the downhill slide was irreversable, Mackay retired from the Comstock in 1883, although he kept major interests until 1895.

The life of an indolent man of leisure did not appeal, though, and he was soon deeply involved in such enterprises as steamships, an early New York subway, and trans-Atlantic cables. With his family on the far side of the ocean, it was this latter project which interested him most. In partnership with James Gordon Bennett of the *New York Herald,* he formed the Commercial Cable Company. A cable was laid across the ocean by this firm in 1884, but as Western Union refused to use it Mackay next founded the Postal Telegraph Company to compete with them. A serious rate war nearly led to financial ruin, but Mackay held on until his company was a viable success.

An assassination attempt on Mackay's life in San Francisco caused a stir throughout the country, although the bullet wound was not critical. Then the death of his eldest son in 1895 brought another huge public outpouring of sentiment. He had planned to turn over management of all his businesses to this son, but now he placed the responsibility on Clarence.

Although declining in health, Mackay attempted to complete one more project — that of laying the first trans-Pacific cable. It was still unfinished when he died in England on July 20, 1902. Estimates of the size of his estate at that time ranged between $30 and $60 million, but his San Francisco business manager stated, "I don't suppose he knew within twenty millions what he was worth." Part of this fortune was returned to Nevada when his son Clarence endowed the Mackay School of Mines at the University of Nevada in Reno in honor of his father. In front of the school today stands a bronze statue of a youthful John Mackay, with a pick at his side, peering intently off to the south — directly at the Comstock Lode.

John Mackay, leader of the "Bonanza Firm."

James G. Fair

Although equally as important as Mackay in the management of the "Bonanza Firm" James Fair was so soundly disliked that upon his death a newspaper editor wrote, "I have yet to hear a good word spoken of him." He, like Mackay, was born in Dublin in 1831, and came to America with his emigrating family when he was about ten years old. In 1849 he left the Illinois farm his family was then working to join the California gold rush.

After two years as a placer miner, with very meager returns, he attempted to operate a farm near Petaluma. However, the lure of the Mother Lode drew him back within six months, this time to the management of a stamp mill. Though he failed in this venture, Fair's lifelong love of machines and mechanical ingenuity began to surface. He located a small but rich gold strike in 1856, after which he constructed a large frame home in Calaveras County. Later speculation hear Angels Camp wiped out much of his profits, although he there met and married Theresa Rooney.

He continued his mine and mill operations in California until 1865, when he supposedly perfected a better milling process for Comstock ore. Only then did he sell his holdings and move to Virginia City, where within a year he was made superintendent of the Ophir mine. His capability as a mine superintendent was never questioned, but his arrogant and boasting attitude discouraged any close friendships. It is likely that he and Mackay entered into their 1868 partnership to gain control of the Hale & Norcross mine because they respected each other's abilities, not because they liked each other.

When Flood and O'Brien were also brought into the operation, the "Bonanza Firm" was off and rolling. They bought two mills in Gold Hill, then ac-

A claim map of the Comstock area. The main lode extended from the Sierra Nevada mine at the north end of Virginia City (upper right) to the Belcher mine in Gold Hill (far left). The main Sutro Tunnel extends vertically from the bottom center, while north

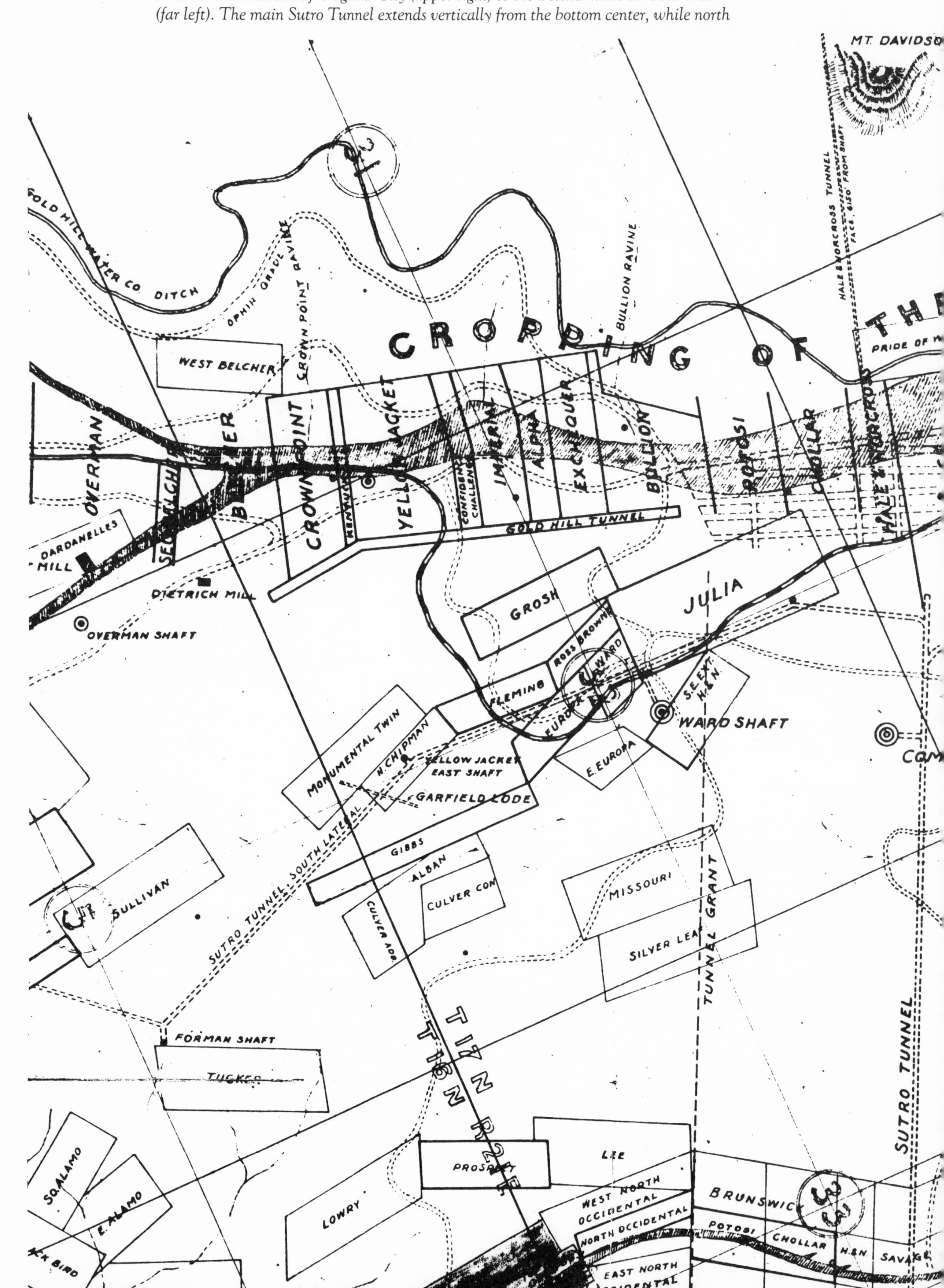

and south lateral tunnels parallel the lode to intersect with all the major mines. Many of the mines shown on this map away from the main lode were non-producers, and some were simply promotional ventures, never having been developed at all.

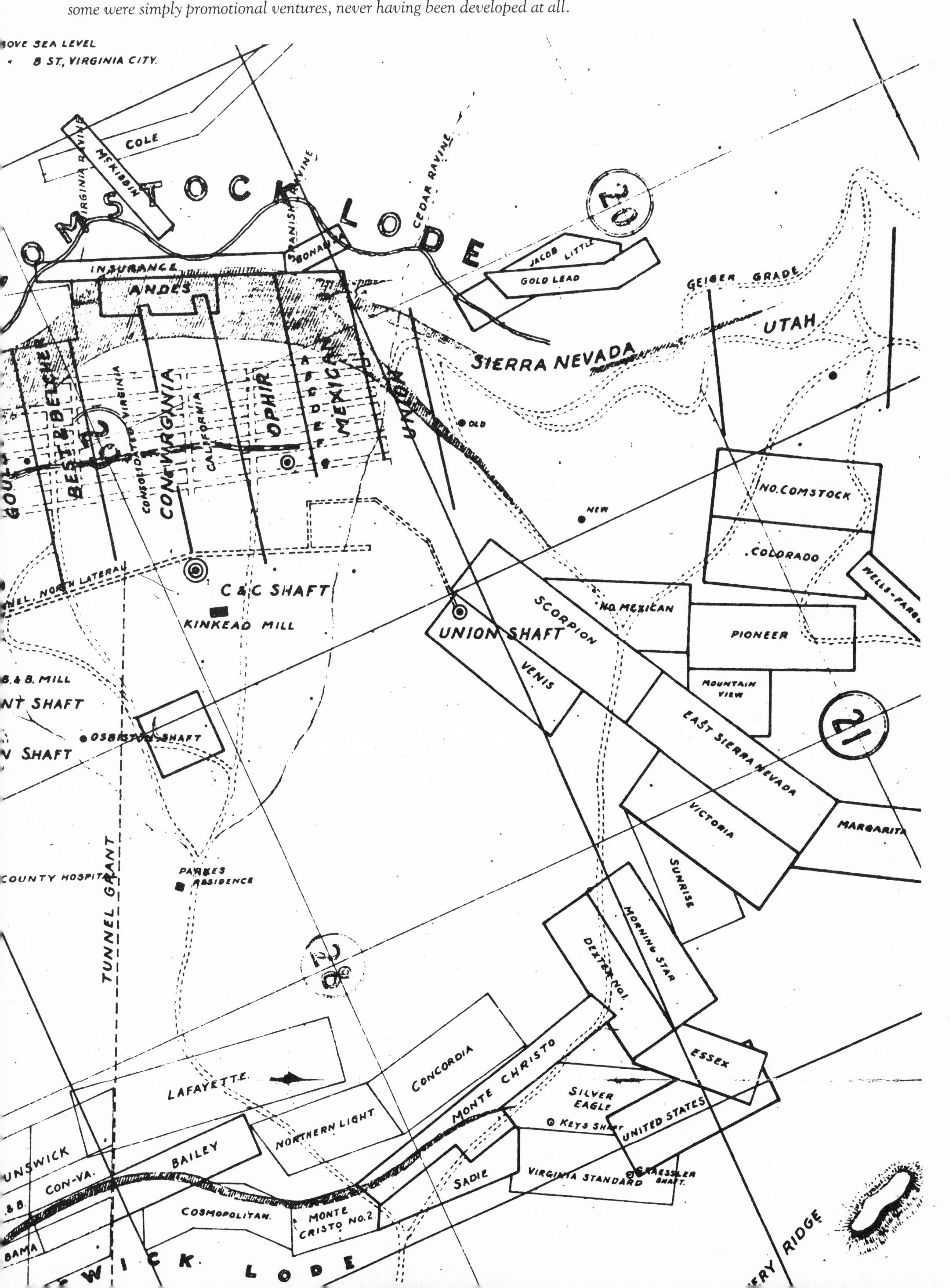

James G. Fair, Mackay's major partner in the "Bonanza Firm."

quired Sharon's interest in the Virginia & Gold Hill Water Company, before Fair decided to engage in another venture of his own. He sunk a great deal of money into the Savage mine before deciding to write it off as a failure in 1871. Again pooling their resources, the Bonanza Firm gained control of the Consolidated Virginia mine in 1871. Fair, of course, claimed credit for the discovery of the "Big Bonanza" two years later, and may indeed be responsible for pursuing the small vein that eventually led to that outstanding orebody.

Both Fair and Mackay took advantage of their positions to make huge profits on stock deals. Mackay's easy-going nature and generosity reduced much of the public stigma this created, but that was not so with Fair. His arrogant manner and less-than-honorable business dealings soon earned him the nickname "Slippery Jim."

By 1879 he could see that the huge profits generated on the Comstock were coming to an end. Not wanting to lose his prominence in the news, and glorying in the new title of "Bonanza King," Fair decided to run against William Sharon for a U.S. Senate seat. The campaign was expensive and hard-fought, but Fair won hands down. However, his six-year term exposed his total inability as a politician, as he spent considerably more time in San Francisco than in Washington. Part of this was due to Fair's constant womanizing, which prompted his wife to file for divorce on the grounds of habitual adultery. The resultant scandal set Fair back, both publicly and financially. The divorce settlement alone was $4.75 million, but it was also the contributing factor in the breakup of the Bonanza Firm.

When Mackay and Flood bought out his share of the Nevada Bank in 1885, he immediately founded the Mutual Savings Bank in California. Fair also purchased the Lick House in San Francisco, where he resided the rest of his life, but business headquarters were in a narrow two-story building on Montgomery Street. His holdings soon included some 60 acres of income property in San Francisco, although his stingy management kept them in a constant state of disrepair. Other holdings encompassed ranches, mines, a substantial portion of a North Beach development, and a railroad between Los Gatos and Santa Cruz. A constantly growing ego, much self-pity, a huge gluttany for food, asthma, and increasing alcoholism had reduced Fair to being a San Francisco eccentric by the early 1890's.

His two daughters, raised by Mrs. Fair after the divorce, both made happy marriages. His two boys, whom he was awarded by the divorce, suffered quite different fates. Alcoholic Jimmy committed suicide in 1891, while spend-thrift Charley and his wife died in an auto crash in France in 1902. Mrs. Fair had died in 1891, leaving her substantial estate to Charley who also contested Fair's will when he died in 1894.

Fair may well be best known for the scandal which erupted after his death. The theft of a will, the appearance of another written in pencil, a previously-unknown marraige contract, and a plethora of persons claiming to be wives or children all added to the confusion. When it was finally settled the Fair estate had been reduced by many millions, while James Fair's true contributions to the development of the Comstock had been far overshadowed by his infamy.

Flood and O'Brien

The two junior partners of the "Bonanza Firm," though still vitally important, had very little to do with the actual operations in Virginia City. James Clair Flood was born of poor Irish immigrants in New York City on October 25, 1826. Nothing is known of his early years until he joined the rush to California in 1849. An accomplished carriage builder, he first worked as a carpenter, then as a placer miner. He made a few thousand dollars, returned to New York in 1851, then bought a farm in Illinois. The lure of the West was too strong, though, and he soon sold out to return to California. He married, opened either a livery stable or a wagon repair shop in San Francisco, then was forced into being a carpenter again when his business went bankrupt.

William Shoney O'Brien, like Mackay and Fair, was born in Dublin and came to America as a child. He worked as a grocery clerk until the 1849 gold rush brought him to California at the age of 23. O'Brien's first partnership was in a newsstand-tobacco shop, then in a ship chandlery. In 1857, when a local depression had him casting around for a new venture, he entered into a partnership with Flood. The two men opened the Auction Lunch saloon on Washington Street, next to a well-patronized produce market.

The business did well, and when the San Francisco Mining Exchange opened in 1862 Flood began study-

James Fair's unassuming residence in Virginia City.

ing the market. By 1868 he felt he had learned enough to go into business as a broker, so the saloon was sold to enable he and O'Brien to open a brokerage office on Montgomery Street. Here they met two young men from Virginia City — Mackay and Fair — who were trying to purchase control of the Hale & Norcross mine. The scheme's success created the Bonanza Firm, with Mackay and Fair managing the properties while Flood and O'Brien handled the partnership's business interests with the San Francisco banks and mining exchanges.

Flood was acquisitive and gaudy, while O'Brien's easy-mannered geniality often was the only peacekeeping force among the partners' strong-willed personalities. After the Con. Virginia made them all wealthy, O'Brien became known as the "Jolly Millionaire," while Flood rapidly spent his money on mansions, carriages, and other costly luxuries.

O'Brien died in 1879, leaving an estate valued at between $12 and $15 million. Flood easily took over all the San Francisco operations as he had always been the more able of the two. When O'Brien had once been asked how he came to possess such wealth, he had simply replied that he had caught the tail of a rising kite and hung on.

In 1881 Flood took over management of the Nevada Bank, in which he and Mackay had bought out Fair by 1885. Two years later he took some time off on account of ill health, appointing George Brander as temporary manager. Brander immediately tried to corner the market in wheat, nearly causing the complete failure of the bank. With this added strain, on top of failing health, Flood died in 1889.

Both Flood and O'Brien were vastly minor characters compared to their partners, yet the success of the Bonanza Firm could not have been so well-accomplished without their assistance. In their meteoric rise from saloon-keepers to millionaire stockbrokers lay the real allure of the Comstock Lode — an American fascination that men could become fabulously wealthy through maniupulation of the stock market.

The Two-Fold Problem of Water

Water was always a severe problem on the Comstock, for two completely opposite reasons. As soon as Virginia City and Gold Hill began to grow in 1859, it was found that there was never a sufficient supply of potable water for homes and businesses. However, it was also found that the deeper the mines were sunk, the more hot, highly-mineralized water flooded into the lower levels. The Comstock had not enough water on the one hand, and entirely too much on the other.

The rapid increase in population occasioned by the "Rush to Washoe" in 1859-60 prompted the creation of both the Virginia Water Company and the Gold Hill Water Company. These two firms utilized natural springs for their supply, then augmented it with water from tunnels driven into Sun Mountain specifically for this purpose. On May 12, 1862, the two businesses were merged under the title of the Virginia & Gold Hill Water Company.

The first iron water mains were laid in Virginia City the following year, but total water available for that city was then only 634 gallons per minute. The Cole Tunnel, driven into the mountain in 1867, somewhat eased the problem by supplying 1,515 gallons per minute, but it also caused other primary water sources to dry up. Poor quality water from the Ophir mine was used to augment the supply during the peak demand, causing continual complaints from residents of both Gold Hill and Virginia City.

There simply was not enough good water in the area of the Comstock to handle the increasing demand. A scheme to bring water from the Sierra Nevada mountains west of Washoe Valley had been proposed as early as 1864, but it had been discarded by engineers as being impractical. However, after the Bonanza Firm of Mackay, Fair, Flood, and O'Brien bought control of the water company in 1869, they brought in Hermann Schussler to figure a way to accomplish this task.

Schussler was Chief Engineer of the water project which supplied San Francisco, and after an intensive preliminary investigation he determined that an inverted siphon could be constructed to bring water from the Sierra Nevada mountains to the Comstock. The fact that such a feat had never before been attempted, nor that pipe had never been constructed to withstand such pressures, seemed of little importance.

The water system, completed in 1873, began at Marlette Lake at an altitude of 7,838 feet, from where a wooden flume 4½ miles long carried water to the head of the pipe. It was the pipe itself which was such a marvel. the 11½-inch diameter iron conduit had a thickness which varied from 6/100ths to 31/100ths of an inch, and each 36-inch section was hand-joined with rivets and lead. The fall from the pipe's inlet to the lowest point of the line at the south end of Washoe Valley was 1,887 vertical feet, generating a pressure of 819 pounds per square inch. This pressure caused the water to be forced up the pipe to the east where it emptied into Five Mile Reservoir, more than 1,500 feet above the pipe's lowest level and 120 feet above the level of Virginia City's main water tank. Including the 5.6 miles of wooden flume from the reservoir to the water tank, the entire system was 21.3 miles long, with the specially-built pipe covering seven of those miles.

It was an engineering wonder — another Comstock first. With 2.2 million gallons of water passing through it daily, the shortage had been eased but demand still outstripped supply. Two additional pipelines were laid alongside the first, one in 1875 and another in 1887, before the problem was completely solved.

The foul water in the mines presented an equally-difficult challenge. Huge quantities of hot water, recorded as high as 157°, had been encountered underground, giving Comstock miners their nickname of "Hot Water Plugs." The Sutro Tunnel had been proposed in the early 1860's to drain off this water, but by the time it was completed in 1878 the major mines had already been extended below the tunnel level.

Pumps were the only answer, but conventional equipment soon proved insufficient. The Cousin Jacks from Cornwall, who were the most expert in deep mining, had already experienced similar conditions in their deep copper mines and had devised a huge pump to combat this problem. By the early 1870's these Cornish Pumps were in use on the Comstock, but of a size and capacity never seen in Cornwall.

An example of a typical pump is one used in the Yellow Jacket mine, which had a vertical shaft more than 3,000 feet deep. The pump had two fly wheels weighing 125 tons, a wooden pump rod 16 by 16 inches and 3,055 feet long, and when in operation raised more than a million gallons of water daily. Similar pumps were installed in other mines, with the Union shaft putting the last in operation in 1879.

With the decline of the Comstock, water problems in the mines intensified. As most of the underground workings were connected to each other, the action of one mine shutting down its pumps placed an additional burden on the others. The Combination was the last mine to operate these large machines, and when they ceased pumping in 1886 the flooding of its 3,250-foot deep shaft brought an end to deep mining on the Lode.

An attempt was made to unwater the northern mines on the Comstock beginning in 1899, but the water level was never lowered more than the 2,700-foot level. At one point 170° water squirted out of drill holes and miners were forced to wear heavy gloves to keep from burning their hands. Enormously high costs forced this project to be abandoned by 1920.

In recent years the portion of the water system which supplies the Comstock was purchased by the State of Nevada, while the mains and storage tanks within Virginia City and Gold Hill are owned and maintained by Storey County. Most of the lower workings of the Comstock mines are flooded, but for potable drinking water Virginia City still relies on the century-old engineering wonder to supply its needs of nearly a million gallons daily.

The Following Regulations have been duly adopted by resolution of the Board of Trustees of the Virginia and Gold Hill Water Company:

1. In all cases of non-payment of the water rent within ten days after presentation of bill, the supply will be cut off, and the water shall not again be let on, either for the present or any subsequent occupant, except upon the payment of the amount due, together with the sum of two dollars.
2. No person or family to supply water in any way to other persons or families.
3. Consumers shall prevent all unnecessary waste of water, and shall make no concealment of the purposes for which it is used.
4. No alteration shall be made in any water pipe or fixture, without first giving notice of the intended alteration at the office of the Company.
5. In all cases where water is to be supplied to several parties or tenants from one connection or tap, the Company contracts only with one of said several parties, and on his default to abide these regulations, and pay the rates, will cut off the connection.
6. Whenever any of these regulations shall be violated, the supply of water will be discontinued, and not resumed until all charges and expenses are satisfied
7. All persons taking water shall keep their service pipes in good repair, at their own expense, and they will be held liable for all damages which may resul from their failure to do so.
8. STREET SPRINKLING WITH HOSE, AND STANDING IRRIGATORS, WILL NOT BE ALLOWED UNDER ANY CIRCUMSTANCES.
9. The Inspector, or other properly authorized officer of the Company, shall be admitted at all reasonable hours to all parts of any premises supplied with the water, to see that these regulations are observed.

From here water was carried to Virginia City by a wooden flume, with this wooden cabin built alongside near the mid-point (above). The specially-constructed pipe for the Comstock water system ended at Five-Mile Reservoir near the Ophir Grade road (below).

Oysters and Champagne

To fully appreciate the opulence that existed on the Comstock at the height of its glory days, one must compare it to the rest of the nation. At a time when laborers were paid from $1 to $2 per day elsewhere, Virginia City miners demanded and got $4 a day. Other wages were commensurately higher, with bootmakers and tinsmiths receiving $5 per day, carpenters getting $6, and masons being paid the unheard-of wage of $8 a day.

For the truly shrewd or lucky, there were many thousands of dollars to be made by investing in the mines themselves. George Hearst began his great fortune during a Comstock boom of the 1860's; Sandy Bowers was transformed overnight from a destitute prospector into the owner of a mine which at one time produced some $10,000 a month; and such millionaires as John Mackay, James Fair, William Sharon, "Lucky" Baldwin, D. O. Mills, and William Ralston all acquired their riches during the 1870's. So much money was produced by the mines that at one point the superintendent of the Gould & Curry was reported to be making $40,000 a year, giving him the distinction of receiving one of the highest wages then paid in the entire nation.

Naturally, when money exists in abundance, countless ways to spend it are soon provided. Although the original mining laws drawn up in 1859 prohibited gambling, it was not long before this form of recreation became common and lucrative. A huge number of saloons — some say as many as 100 in Virginia City alone — were patronized day and night. The Comstock theatres were frequently sold out, with the audience delighting in tossing coins on the stage after any pleasing performance.

Some of the very wealthy were not content with building mansions and ornate mine offices, but were known to order silver and gold trimmings for their carriages, put silver shoes on favorite horses, and give away small silver ingots as gifts. This lavish spending extended even to the common miners, who were particularly fond of consuming the traditional Comstock treat of champagne and fresh oysters. So many of these shellfish were freighted over from California packed in ice that great mounds of empty oyster shells were still visible at the old municipal dump in Virginia City as late as the 1970's.

When the second International hotel opened on C Street in 1863, it set a trend for splendor that was

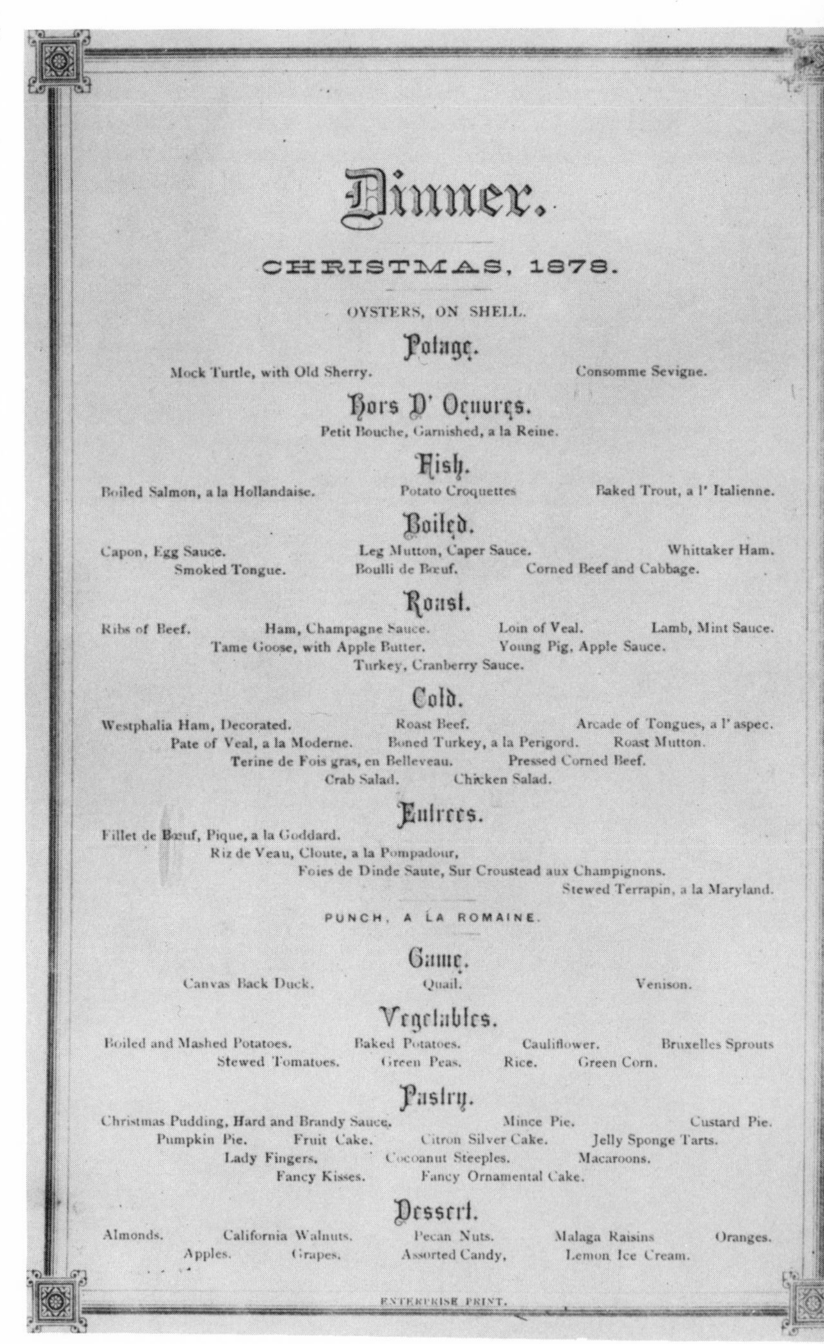

Dinner.

CHRISTMAS, 1878.

OYSTERS, ON SHELL.

Potage.

Mock Turtle, with Old Sherry. Consomme Sevigne.

Hors D' Oeuvres.

Petit Bouche, Garnished, a la Reine.

Fish.

Boiled Salmon, a la Hollandaise. Potato Croquettes Baked Trout, a l' Italienne.

Boiled.

Capon, Egg Sauce. Leg Mutton, Caper Sauce. Whittaker Ham.
Smoked Tongue. Boulli de Bœuf. Corned Beef and Cabbage.

Roast.

Ribs of Beef. Ham, Champagne Sauce. Loin of Veal. Lamb, Mint Sauce.
Tame Goose, with Apple Butter. Young Pig, Apple Sauce.
Turkey, Cranberry Sauce.

Cold.

Westphalia Ham, Decorated. Roast Beef. Arcade of Tongues, a l' aspec.
Pate of Veal, a la Moderne. Boned Turkey, a la Perigord. Roast Mutton.
Terine de Fois gras, en Belleveau. Pressed Corned Beef.
Crab Salad. Chicken Salad.

Entrees.

Fillet de Bœuf, Pique, a la Goddard.
Riz de Veau, Cloute, a la Pompadour,
Foies de Dinde Saute, Sur Croustead aux Champignons.
Stewed Terrapin, a la Maryland.

PUNCH, A LA ROMAINE.

Game.

Canvas Back Duck. Quail. Venison.

Vegetables.

Boiled and Mashed Potatoes. Baked Potatoes. Cauliflower. Bruxelles Sprouts
Stewed Tomatoes. Green Peas. Rice. Green Corn.

Pastry.

Christmas Pudding, Hard and Brandy Sauce. Mince Pie. Custard Pie.
Pumpkin Pie. Fruit Cake. Citron Silver Cake. Jelly Sponge Tarts.
Lady Fingers. Cocoanut Steeples. Macaroons.
Fancy Kisses. Fancy Ornamental Cake.

Dessert.

Almonds. California Walnuts. Pecan Nuts. Malaga Raisins Oranges.
Apples. Grapes. Assorted Candy, Lemon Ice Cream.

ENTERPRISE PRINT.

At this well patronized Comstock saloon, beer was delivered in wooden barrels, such as the man in the rear is straddling, but bar stools had yet to appear in western saloons. The International hotel's 1878 Christmas menu featured such choices as eight different kinds of champagne, while oysters are prominently offered at the very top of the bill of fare.

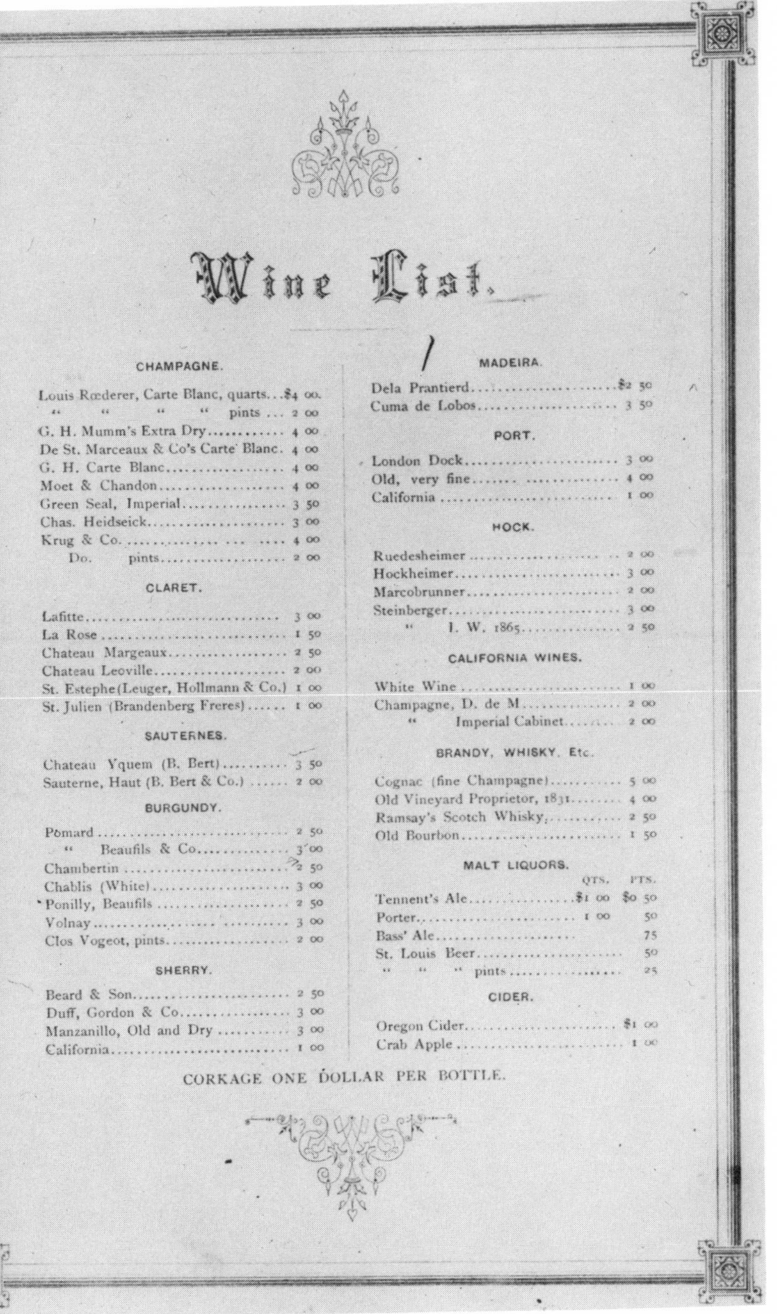

Wine List.

CHAMPAGNE.

Louis Rœderer, Carte Blanc, quarts	$4 00
" " " " pints	2 00
G. H. Mumm's Extra Dry	4 00
De St. Marceaux & Co's Carte Blanc	4 00
G. H. Carte Blanc	4 00
Moet & Chandon	4 00
Green Seal, Imperial	3 50
Chas. Heidseick	3 00
Krug & Co.	4 00
Do. pints	2 00

CLARET.

Lafitte	3 00
La Rose	1 50
Chateau Margeaux	2 50
Chateau Leoville	2 00
St. Estephe (Leuger, Hollmann & Co.)	1 00
St. Julien (Brandenberg Freres)	1 00

SAUTERNES.

Chateau Yquem (B. Bert)	3 50
Sauterne, Haut (B. Bert & Co.)	2 00

BURGUNDY.

Pomard	2 50
" Beaufils & Co.	3 00
Chambertin	2 50
Chablis (White)	3 00
Ponilly, Beaufils	2 50
Volnay	3 00
Clos Vogeot, pints	2 00

SHERRY.

Beard & Son	2 50
Duff, Gordon & Co.	3 00
Manzanillo, Old and Dry	3 00
California	1 00

MADEIRA.

Dela Prantierd	$2 50
Cuma de Lobos	3 50

PORT.

London Dock	3 00
Old, very fine	4 00
California	1 00

HOCK.

Ruedesheimer	2 00
Hockheimer	3 00
Marcobrunner	2 00
Steinberger	3 00
" I. W. 1865	2 50

CALIFORNIA WINES.

White Wine	1 00
Champagne, D. de M	2 00
" Imperial Cabinet	2 00

BRANDY, WHISKY, Etc.

Cognac (fine Champagne)	5 00
Old Vineyard Proprietor, 1831	4 00
Ramsay's Scotch Whisky	2 50
Old Bourbon	1 50

MALT LIQUORS.

	QTS.	PTS.
Tennent's Ale	$1 00	$0 50
Porter	1 00	50
Bass' Ale		75
St. Louis Beer		50
" " " pints		25

CIDER.

Oregon Cider	$1 00
Crab Apple	1 00

CORKAGE ONE DOLLAR PER BOTTLE.

unmatched in any other community of comparable size. It was soon followed by such establishments as the Washoe Club, with its private smoking, billiard, card, and reading rooms. French restaurants, German beerhalls, and dozens of assorted eateries provided every type of culinary treat imaginable. Wild game was served in a dozen different ways, fresh fish was usually available from California, and so much beefsteak was consumed that it became common to see men dining on it for breakfast.

As well as spending lavishly to indulge their own wants, Comstockers were prone to feats of generosity. When Gridley's flour sack was repeatedly auctioned to raise funds for the Sanitary Commission during the Civil War, Gold Hill and Virginia City competed to see which community could donate the greater amount of money. Members of the Miners' Union gladly contributed from their wages to supply necessary funds for an injured miner, as well as seeing to the financial wants of the family of any man killed in the mines. Public subscriptions accounted for the revenue needed to establish the first schools, as well as founding and supplying the Comstock's two public libraries. It was also the lavish and often anonymous donations which built the churches of the area and St. Mary's hospital.

Grant Smith in his history of the Comstock Lode perhaps stated the tenor of the times best when he wrote, "Everybody continued to take part in the endless celebrations and social events. Life was still a great adventure... A more self-reliant, independent, brave, and generous community of men and women did not exist. The world was young and they thought themselves fortunate to be living at such a time." *(Nev. Bur. of Mines & Geo. Bull. 37)*

Ships of the Desert

As early as 1848, Colonel Crossman of the U.S. Army had assigned Major Henry Wayne to investigate the possibility of using camels in the Far West. Little was done at that time, but when Jefferson Davis was Chairman of the Committee on Military Affairs in 1851 he used every means to effect the founding of a "Camel Corps." Four years later, when Secretary of War Davis was still lobbying for a true experiment with camels, Congress finally appropriated $30,000 for such an experiment. He was hoping to open better communications between the South and California.

The first shipload of 33 camels and dromedaries, all purchased or presented to the U.S. in the Mid-East, were unloaded at Indianola, Texas in June, 1856. The specially-modified ship used to transport them set sail for another load, disembarking 41 more animals early in 1857. With this nucleus a permanent training camp was established north of San Antonio, and "Uncle Sam's Camel Corps" became a reality.

Camels are difficult animals at best, so to the precision-trained dragoons assigned to them they must have been enormously difficult to master. Reports tell of injuries from bites and kicks, motion sickness from riding their unusual gait, and injuries to the camels from improper handling and packing. All was eventually straightened out, as Lt. Edward Beale used the animals in opening a new wagon road from Texas to California.

With the advent of the Civil War in 1861, the last thing Washington wanted was easier access between the southern states and the goldfields of California. The camels were put in a holding facility in Los Angeles to free the dragoons for service elsewhere, then the animals were transferred to Benicia in 1863. When the idea of a "camel corps" was completely abandoned, it was decided to sell the camels at public auction.

The sale took place in February, 1864, with Samuel McLanaghan purchasing the entire herd. He then sold three to a circus, shipping the rest to his ranch in Sonoma County which he hoped to use as a base for camel pack trains to Nevada. To raise money for this venture a "Great Dromedary Race" was staged in Sacramento. The affair proved to be a failure, but it did provide spectators with a view of the first American camel race.

His camels were eventually used in Nevada, as well as in Arizona and as far north as British Columbia.

Virginia City's modern National Championship Camel Races feature local and celebrity riders on the gentle-appearing animals (below). Yet in a matter of seconds the 2,000-pound camels can be transformed into some of the most difficult animals to handle.

Pack trains using camels hauled salt, firewood, and freight in Nevada — one small train even being used to haul wood for the huge July 4, 1876, bonfire on top of Sun Mountain above the Comstock.

Camels also caused a problem, however. Their strange appearance, odors, and sounds would often spook horses into bolting or overturning carriages, causing numerous accidents. Virginia City first banned their entry into town during the daytime, then the State of Nevada passed a law in 1875 prohibiting their use on any road or highway. Eventually all the camels were sold to persons outside of Nevada or were turned loose to fend for themselves. The elements took their toll, with the last sighting of a camel in Nevada occurring early in this century.

Some twenty years ago a Virginia City newspaper editor wrote a humorous but totally false story about the results of a just-completed camel race on the Comstock. The following year, however, he made the mistake of announcing the fictitious race before it was to have occurred. He was immediately presented with a challenge from a competitor, who arrived in Virginia City with a pair of camels! The race was run, and it has become an annual event.

The unusual sight of a pair of 2,000-pound camels racing down E Street is a very real part of the Comstock's summer activities. Less well known, but still sworn to by some, are the legends of a huge red camel said to roam the slopes of Sun Mountain on nights the Washoe Zephyr is blowing, and the tale of a ghost camel train wandering aimlessly in the salt flat southeast of the mouth of Six-Mile Canyon. Ghost stories notwithstanding, camels were a very real means of transportation in early-day Nevada, fitting right in with all the incongruities that made Virginia City so unique.

Stock Swindles

THE SILVER MANIA AT SAN FRANCISCO.

Total production of the Comstock mines has been accurately estimated at very near $400 million, making them some of the richest mines in the U.S. Yet high operating costs and occasional depressions in the prices of silver and gold combined to reduce profits to only a small portion of this production. To illustrate this, only 19 of the 400-odd mining companies formed on the Comstock between 1859 and 1880 paid any dividends to their shareholders, yet every one of the 400 levied assessments on their shares.

Private profits made off these mines totaled only $20 million, but at least 29 men are reported to have made in excess of $1 million on the Comstock. Some of these men did make money from actual mine production, although they were relatively few in number. Most of these personal fortunes, and many others amounting to less than a million dollars, were instead made by investing in mining company stock, which gave rise to an atmosphere of swindling and false promotion unlike any which had occurred before.

Some mining companies would secure a piece of barren ground, issue stock, and levy an assessment or two. The principals would then dissolve the company, leaving stockholders with share certificates "not worth a dollar a cord." In other cases mines were salted to induce investors to purchase stock, and in some instances to buy entire mines. A contemporary historian wrote that "silver was melted into the rock or plugged in, in such a way as to resemble natural ores, so that a person not an expert would see silver all around in a worthless mine."

But the real money, involving many thousands of dollars, was made buying and selling shares in legitimate, operating mines. Suppose a small businessman in San Francisco had invested $100 in July, 1870, by purchasing Con. Virginia stock when it was $1 a share. Three and a half years later, in December, 1874, that stock had risen to $610 a share, netting the investor a profit of $60,900. In reality, small investors seldom hung onto their stock for any length of time, but it was this dream which prompted so many persons to gamble so heavily in mining shares.

Unfortunately, the price of mining stock often rose or fell through manipulation, often generated only by rumor and innuendo, rather than as a reflection of the mine's worth. The best recorded example occurred in 1872, when Savage mine stock was inflated from $62 a share to $725. Superintendent Alvinza Hayward first offered to buy unlimited quantities of stock, immediately creating curiosity as to his motives. Since he and his partner, John P. Jones, were in control of the Savage, they next closed the mine. The public was not allowed in, and the miners were confined inside for several days, unable to confirm or deny the rumors that a big strike had been made. The rapid rise of Savage stock carried other Comstock mine shares up with it. Crown Point stock rose to $1,825 while shares in the Belcher climbed to $1,525. The inevitable finally occurred early in May, and the ensuing crash saw Comstock mining stock fall 30 to 40 percent. Hayward and a few others made a great deal of money on this escapade, but thousands of small investors were wiped out.

Another widespread form of swindling was practiced by unscrupulous stockbrokers who "shorted" their clients' stocks. The broker, who was holding the shares for his client, would collect the assessments when they were levied but would not pay them to the mining company.

Still another brokers' trick was to "bucket" clients' orders. The investor would give a purchase order for so many shares of a certain mine on margin, depositing a percentage of the cost with the broker. However, the broker often failed to buy the shares, but instead pocketed the deposit. He would collect the interest due on the client's note, as well as all monies due on any assessments that were levied by the company, even though his client actually owned no shares at all. This was especially common in a depressed market, where the broker felt assured that he could purchase the stated shares whenever he wished and probably at a lower price than at the time of the original order.

The practice had grown so widespread by 1886 that James L. Flood, son of the Bonanza Firm's James Flood, decided to create a situation to wipe out some of these unscrupulous brokers. The Comstock mines were very depressed at that time, with Con. Virginia selling for $2.50 a share. On October 16 the Combination shaft was closed, which signalled the end of deep mining on the Lode. But instead of falling, Comstock shares began to increase in value. Word soon spread that someone had been buying Comstock mining stock as quickly as it came on the market. That someone was Flood, and a few other mine managers who were in on the deal. Con. Virginia rose to $62 by early December, and once again the public began investing heavily in Comstock mines, hoping to get in on the boom.

By December 11 it was estimated that almost $4 million had been pumped into these shares by private individuals. Brokers who had been "shorting" or "bucketing" their clients' orders were suddenly called upon to deliver, but with the rapidly rising market it was impossible for them to purchase the shares they had supposedly bought long ago. Many of the Virginia City and San Francisco stockbrokers failed, and the San Francisco Stock Exchange was forced to close for a day as a result of the turmoil. When the elder James Flood returned from the East, he decided that the scheme had gone far enough. The following day Con. Virginia fell to $32 a share, with the rest of the market tumbling down with it. The "1886 Deal," as it soon became known, did accomplish the objective of punishing some of the rotten brokers, but it also broke the public's confidence in Comstock mines. Thirty years of swindling and manipulations had taken their toll, for never again would Comstock mining stock rise to such heights on unsubstantiated claims.

Many men did indeed make great fortunes in the buying and selling of these mining stocks, but only at the expense of countless thousands of little investors. On the whole, though, men of that era considered the market to be a game of chance not much different from a roulette wheel or a poker table. Eliot Lord stated in 1883 that the San Francisco exchanges "had become gambling establishments of a low order," yet it would take another 45 years before the American dream of reaping quick fortunes in the stock market would finally come to a crashing halt.

Perhaps as an indication of approval of some of the shady "deals" which have been perpetrated in Virginia City, the statue of Justice on the Storey County courthouse is one of the few in the nation which is not blindfolded.

1876 Nevada Medallion

Besides being the peak year of Virginia City's "Big Bonanza" period, 1876 was also the 100th anniversary of the nation. An enormous exposition was held at Philadelphia to commemorate the Centennial, and naturally the first and greatest of all U.S. silver mining towns was not to be left out. A special Nevada Building was erected immediately behind Machinery Hall on the exposition grounds to house a fully-operational 5-stamp quartz mill, large displays of mineral specimens, and the most modern mining equipment.

Since demonstration runs were frequently made on the quartz mill, an appropriate use had to be found for the silver that was refined. A special commemorative medallion was decided upon, with U.S. Mint engraver William Barber being contracted to prepare a suitable design on the dies. The Con. Virginia, California, Belcher, and Ophir mines sent 48 tons of ore to Philadelphia, and from its reduction came the silver used in the medallions. The surplus was later sold by the mine owners.

A total of 2,524 medallions were struck at the Philadelphia Mint and offered for sale at the Nevada Building. Priced at $1.25 each, the exact number sold is unknown but only a small number were remelted at the close of the six-month exposition. The medallion sales, coupled with other revenue generated at the Nevada Building, returned more than $4,000 to the Nevada State Board of Centennial Commissioners to help offset the expenses incurred in setting up the exhibit.

The exceptional beauty of the obverse die prompted its use as the reverse of the 1976 Nevada State Bicennial Medallion. Comstock ore was unavailable for use in this latter piece, but it was struck on an 1870's coin press in the Nevada State Museum located in the old Carson City Mint building.

The 1876 Nevada Medallion shows the design created by William Barber on the obverse (left) and the Nevada State Seal on the reverse (right).

Bishop Manogue

This carte de visite *of Father Patrick Manogue was taken in the late 1860's, near the time he was made Vicar General of the Diocese.*

In the early days of Virginia City, when churches were few and far between, it took men of great determination and stamina to bring religion to this turbulent area. Luckily there were men of this character to fill the bill and by far the most famous in all of Nevada was Bishop Manogue.

Born in 1831 in County Kilkenney, Ireland, Patrick Manogue was 18 years old when he emigrated to the United States. After a two-year stay in Connecticut, he managed to attend four years at Chicago's University of St. Mary's of the Lake. Further education would cost more than he could afford, so Manogue went where there was money to be made. From 1854 until 1857 he worked as a laborer in the gold mines near Moore's Flat, California, and salted away every dollar he could. When enough had been accumulated, he sailed for France to spend four more years in the Seminary of St. Sulpice at Paris. Finally, on December 21, 1861, Patrick Manogue was ordained a priest in the Roman Catholic Church. Six months later, in June, 1862, he arrived in Virginia City.

To say that Nevada Territory was then "unsettled" would be an understatement. The Civil War then raging in the East was affecting sentiments and politics even in the Far West. At the same time miners were just beginning to organize the first unions to demand better pay and working conditions. Law and order were limited in many areas of the state, and inter-racial conflicts were constantly brewing.

Father Manogue saw it all. Standing 6′3″ and weighing 250 pounds, he was constantly traveling throughout Nevada to preach, organize, marry, baptize, minister to the sick, give the last rites, and conduct services for the dead. He once rode 180 miles to comfort a man sentenced to be hanged, but when he arrived he was soon convinced of the man's innocence. He immediately rode the same distance back to Carson City in the dead of winter, demanded to see Governor Nye, and obtained a pardon for the condemned man.

At other times he was forced to disarm an enraged husband who refused the administering of the last rites to his dying wife; stood fast before a lynch mob determined to hang a miner named Bonner; settled serious disputes between the miners and the Chinese; and was always the mainstay of relief in such disasters as the great fire of 1875 and the fatal underground fires of the Yellow Jacket and Belcher mines.

And all the while he was building. As soon as he arrived in Virginia City in 1862, he ordered the building of the first Catholic Church there which cost $12,000. Named St. Mary's of the Mountains, it was soon too small for the ever-growing congregation and a new brick church costing $65,000 was built in 1868. It was completely destroyed in the fire of 1875 whereupon the magnificent church standing today was erected upon the rubble of the old.

In 1863 he also organized the St. Vincent de Paul Society in Virginia City and the following year began construction of St. Mary's School for girls and St. Vincent's School for boys. In 1875, aided by the financial generosity of Mr. and Mrs. John Mackay, Father Manogue also built the brick St. Mary's Hospital.

His work for the church did not go unrewarded. In 1868 he was made Vicar General of the Diocese of Grass Valley, which included the Virginia City parish and all the rest of the State of Nevada, and in 1880 was named Bishop of the Diocese. He was still serving in this capacity when he died in Sacramento in 1895, and a parochial high school in Reno has been named in his memory.

Towns of the Comstock Lode

American City

Located near the center of American Flat, approximately two miles northwest of Silver City, American City was laid out in January, 1864. The founding fathers were men of means, and immediately offered a bribe of $50,000 to the territorial coffers if the capitol were relocated from Carson City to their new community. A heated debate ensued, with all of Storey County in favor of the move while most of the rest of Nevada opposed it. The capitol stayed in Carson City, but American City enjoyed a few years of activity without it.

Various businesses, including two hotels, were operated during the mid-1860's. A post office was established in 1866, but the settlement started to decline the following year. The post office was discontinued in February, 1868, with the town's abandonment occurring soon afterward.

Comstock

In 1920, at a time when mining on the Comstock had reached a low ebb, the United Comstock Mines Company was incorporated to work many of the Gold Hill properties. A $1.5 million cyanide mill was constructed in American Flat, near the head of American Ravine, while a 9,250-foot adit was dug north to intersect the Imperial mine on its 700-foot level. A two-mile spur of the V&T RR was also laid to the complex. The company town of Comstock was located north and west of the mill, serving to house first the construction workers building the project then the employees' homes, a store, and other company buildings after the plant went into operation.

Three years later the venture had produced $3.4 million, but high expenses had reduced the profits to practically nothing. The entire operation was sold to Comstock Merger Mines, Inc., who operated the mill until 1927. It was then shut down, the equipment removed and sold to a California firm, and the mining property sold to the Sutro Coalition Company. The post office, which had been established in 1923, was closed in February, 1927, as the short-lived community was abandoned.

Dayton

The grassy flat bounded by cottonwoods, where Gold Canyon empties into the Carson River, was a frequent camping spot for California-bound emigrants. Some of these paused to work the placers, especially one group of Mormons which returned from California to mine here, and a party of Mexicans also arrived until about 100 men were working in the canyon in 1850. So many emigrants used the Carson River route to California in 1850 that they depleted all supplies and foodstuffs. Relief parties had to be sent back over the Sierra from California to aid the Gold Canyon miners. The placers were abandoned for the winter, on account of shortages, so it was not until 1851 that a permanent settlement was created.

A tent trading post was erected, then replaced in late 1853 by a better-stocked wooden structure. By 1858 many of the residents had followed the placer diggings as they were worked ever higher up Gold Canyon until all that remained were just a few people. A group of Orientals living nearby worked placer claims in the area, though not where Caucasians were mining, and were also hired to dig the Rose Ditch from the Carson River to some placer ground low in the canyon. From them the community became known as Chinatown, although Mark Twain's brother Orion wrote in August, 1861, that it was also called Nevada City.

When Nevada Territory was created the population felt a more fitting name than Chinatown was needed. The community was officially renamed Dayton at a public meeting on November 3, 1861, and it was also chosen as the county seat when Lyon County was created 26 days later. A post office was established in January, with the number of residents continuing to grow as Dayton became an important milling center. By 1864 it was a serious contender for the location of the capitol, with its population reported at 2,500 the following year.

A serious fire in 1866 destroyed much of the town, after which the population dwindled considerably. The construction of the Sutro Tunnel in the 1870's brought a moderate surge of activity, with the town's

The Dayton hotel was a popular meeting place for local residents of the 19th century. The view of Dayton looking south shows the river and the large number of trees, which helped make this community one of the most pleasant in western Nevada.

Here is a very rare view of Devil's Gate, showing the toll-road which led up Gold Canyon. During the early years prior to the construction of the railroad, this road would be crammed day and night with teams and wagons handling the massive amount of freight needed to supply the Comstock and to haul ore to the mills. As this photo was taken on July 4, 1862, nearly everyone in the region was attending the celebrations in Virginia City, which is why the normally busy road is temporarily empty.

quartz mills expanding to a total of 180 stamps. However, by the time the Carson & Colorado Railroad was built through Dayton in 1881, its population had again shrunk to only 200 persons.

It remained fairly stable until 1909, when two separate fires in May destroyed both the 56-stamp Nevada Reduction Works and the Lyon County courthouse. The latter was not rebuilt, and the county seat was moved to Yerington in 1911. Floating dredges were brought in to work the Gold Canyon placers in the early 1920's, and sporadic mining continued through the 1940's, leaving mounds of gravel even at the edge of town.

Today Dayton's population is again growing, due mainly to its proximity to Carson City. A number of 19th century buildings are still preserved and occupied, although a fire in 1981 leveled the famous old Union hotel building in the center of town. As the second oldest continuously occupied community in Nevada, Dayton still retains picturesque qualities reminiscent of a century ago.

Devil's Gate

The rock formation known as Devil's Gate, through which pass both Gold Canyon and the main road to Virginia City from the south, was a noted early-day landmark. In the summer of 1850 the first prospect shaft in the region was sunk here. It also lent its name to the early Devil's Gate & Chinatown Mining District, and served as the foundation upon which the little stone fort was erected against possible Indian attack in 1860. The rock formation was also a feature on the line dividing Storey and Lyon Counties, but was perhaps best known as the natural gatepost for a toll road.

The actual community, separate from both Silver City and Gold Hill, began to develop in late 1859 or early 1860. By 1881 it contained several saloons, two hotels, two stables, two shoe shops, a brewery, express office, barber, blacksmith, general store, butcher shop, and a few mines and mills. However, the community was also reported to have "partaken of the general recent dullness." That condition intensified as the bonanza years came to an end, producing complete abandonment before the end of the century.

Divide

When Virginia City and Gold Hill were still relatively small towns, a separate community began to develop on the ridge between the two settlements. Sometimes known as Middletown, the area was usually called the Divide, claiming a peak population of around 1,000 during the 1870's.

The Divide never had a separate community

government, nor even a distinct business district. It is perhaps most well known as the spot where Mark Twain was robbed one night, as nothing else of note ever happened here. Today it is considered a part of Virginia City and is the site of a growing residential district.

Dutch Nick's (in Six-Mile Canyon)

Two different locations have been the site of a Dutch Nick's, both the property of one Nicholas Ambrosia. His first station and saloon was built on the banks of the Carson River in 1855. Although he was illiterate, Dutch Nick was appointed Justice of the Peace of Carson County that year, having to acknowledge this appointment by making his mark, since he couldn't write.

About two years later he abandoned that property to take up residence in Johntown. During the summer months he would operate a combination saloon and restaurant in Six-Mile Canyon, charging the miners in the area $14 a week for board. It was this location that O'Riley and McLaughlin frequented while working the placers that would lead them to the discovery of the Comstock Lode.

When Gold Hill was founded in 1859, Dutch Nick moved his Johntown structure to the new location, thus claiming the honor of owning the first building in that town. But when the "Rush to Washoe" developed later that year, he moved back to the site of his original location on the Carson River, which became part of the town of Empire City in 1860. Dutch Nick operated a hotel on its main street for many years. Unfortunately, the site of his Six-Mile Canyon operation is today unknown.

Empire City

With the discovery of the Comstock in 1859, and the subsequent need to have quartz reduction mills located near reliable souces of water, mills began to be built along the Carson River. Near there in March, 1860, the Empire City townsite was laid out 3½ miles east of Carson City where the Emigrant Trail, Overland Stage route, and Pony Express route came within a short distance of the river.

The town grew rapidly, until by the middle of the decade it was a half mile by three-quarters of a mile in size and populated with 700 people. Numerous quartz mills were built not only within the town itself, but extending up and down the river for some distance. When the V&T RR was completed from Virginia City to Carson in 1869, the milling business diverted to Empire City was so great that it caused the abandonment of the town of Ophir and drastically hurt the economy of Washoe City.

Besides quartz mills, numerous lumber mills and woodyards were also constructed at Empire. Timber was cut in the mountains to the west, then floated down to the mills in giant rafts which were sometimes four miles in length. However, the V&T's construction of their own woodyard south of Carson in 1870 cut into the timber business at Empire, although 50,000 cords of wood still went through this community in 1880.

The decline of the Comstock mines which began in the late 1870's led to a reduction of all related industry. The population of Empire diminished to 150 by 1880, and at the turn of the century it was nearly abandoned. The post office, which had been established in 1866, was closed in 1910. When the last of the Carson River mills shut down early in the 20th century, the town died. However, with the increased traffic on U.S. highway 50, a community known as New Empire began to develop a half mile from "old" Empire City. Today all that remains of the original town are earth scars where the major mills once thrived.

Five Mile House

One of the three stations on the 1863 Geiger Grade was Five Mile House, located a mile north of Summit House in a level area known as Five Mile Flat. Very little is known about this station, due in part to the fact that some historians have confused it with Summit House. The actual dates of its inception and abandonment are lost, but it was from this site that construction work on the new Geiger Grade was begun in 1935.

Flowery

The Flowery Mining District, some 3½ miles down Six-Mile Canyon, was the scene of low-grade placer mining as early as 1858. Following the discovery of the Comstock Lode a number of claims were staked in 1860, but only the Lady Bryan proved to be of any value. A small community called Flowery existed here for a short time during the early 1860's. When the other mines proved unproductive, the only residents who remained were employed in or directly involved with the Lady Bryan mine until it suspended operations in 1881.

The discovery of the Flowery mine in 1918, and the resumption of mining in the Lady Bryan, brought a small number of men into the area. Today only exploratory work is being done, with the area closed to the public.

The V&T RR yard in Gold Hill, showing wood being transferred from railroad flatcars to wagons being pulled by six-horse hitches.

Gold Hill

Throughout the mid-1850's dozens of placer miners slowly worked their way up Gold Canyon. When winter set in each year they would abandon their diggings for the lower altitudes but in January, 1859, a nice spell of warm weather occurred. To get in a few more days of mining, John Bishop, Old Virginny, Alexander Henderson, and John Yount set out to investigate a little mound of promising ground high in the canyon. The first pan each man worked contained between eight and fifteen cents worth of gold, a very good showing. The men christened the place Gold Hill, each of the discoverers staking a 50 by 400-foot claim. A few days later the locators showed the site to Henry Comstock, James Rogers, Sandy Bowers, Joe Plato, and William Knight. These last five staked one 50 by 400-foot claim, giving each locator 10 feet of the ground.

The return of bad weather kept the men from

working the area, but by April the placers were in operation. As soon as the new diggings were shown to be extremely rich, most of the Johntown residents picked up and moved to Gold Hill. Among the first structures was a log boardinghouse and restaurant built by Eilley Orrum, the future Mrs. Sandy Bowers. Then followed a frame grocery store owned by Sol Weihl, numerous tents, cabins, dugouts, and even brush shanties.

In June the Comstock Lode was discovered, prompting the founding of Virginia City and the start of the mad rush to "Washoe." By August, 1860, Gold Hill had grown to include 179 structures and 638 residents, of which 14 were women. It continued to grow, and five months later claimed a population of 1,294. On December 17, 1862, the community was incorporated by an Act of the Territorial Legislature.

Virginia City had been named the county seat when Storey County was created in 1861, giving rise to a constant rivalry between the two neighboring towns. By 1863 feelings had risen to a fever pitch when the Legislature attempted to consolidate all the communities within the county under one municipal government. As Virginia City was so much larger than Gold Hill, it would effectively place control of these towns under the rule of that city. This was unthinkable to the residents of Gold Hill, who countered by introducing a bill in the 1864 Legislature to create a separate county, of which they would naturally have the county seat. Eventually the furor died away, leaving the major towns with their own governments but still within the one county, although the rivalry between Gold Hill and Virginia City continued in many other ways for decades.

By 1865 Gold Hill was a lively town with three foundries, three fraternal organizations, two newspapers, two banks, four stage offices, a large business section, and three churches, although the latter had few members. Four years later the construction of the V&T RR through town brought an even greater period of prosperity, lasting for nearly a decade.

Millions were taken out of the Gold Hill mines during the 1870's, principally from the Belcher, Confidence, Crown Point, Imperial, Kentuck, and Yellow Jacket. Then with the overall decline of the Comstock Lode in the last years of the decade, the area began to suffer. The *Gold Hill News*, the town's last and most famous newspaper, ceased operations in 1882, followed by the inexorable closing of mines and businesses.

A brief resurgence occurred early in this century when the United Comstock operation began in nearby American Flat. Some open pit mining was also done in the area, but it was not enough to keep the town alive. The railroad through Gold Hill was abandoned in 1938, the 81-year old post office was closed in 1943, and the community became a virtual ghost town.

The modern tourist boom after 1950, with its resultant increase in population on the Comstock, brought new life to Gold Hill. Some of the remaining homes were beautifully restored, new ones were built, and the town now has two saloons, a hotel, and a few small shops. The *Gold Hill News* was reactivated for a few years during the 1970's, recapturing much of the flavor of 19th century journalism, but it has since folded. The expansion of the Imperial pit by Houston Oil & Minerals nearly brought about the destruction of a number of historic homes and the rerouting of the highway through town. At the last moment a reprieve was granted when the open pit mine shut down, coinciding with a fall in the price of precious metals. While it is still much smaller than Virginia City, Gold Hill nevertheless retains the character of an early-day mining community.

Johntown

In 1851 Old Virginny moved some two miles above the mouth of Gold Canyon where he made his home in a tent-roofed dugout. While this could be construed as the founding of Johntown, it was not until Walter Cosser opened the first store there in 1853 that the community began to take shape. The following year another store was opened by J. S. Child and Moses Job. With the growing numbers of miners in Gold Canyon most goods had to be freighted over the Sierra from California to meet the demand, necessitating high prices. During the winter of 1854 coffee sold for 45¢ a pound, tea $1.25 a pound, tobacco brought $1.50 per pound, wool shirts were between $3 and $4 each, leather boots sold for $5 to $14, and rubber boots commanded $25 a pair.

When Brigham Young in 1857 demanded that Mormons living in outlying regions return to Salt Lake City many chose to defy their church by remaining in the area. A large number did heed the call however, leaving Johntown without a single store when their Mormon owners headed eastward. The vacancies left by the Mormon departure were soon filled by additional emigrants, making Johntown the most prominent mining community in western Utah Territory during the next two years. In 1854 the first newspaper in what is now Nevada was published here, although each issue was only a hand-written single sheet.

Johntown, in Gold Canyon below Silver City, was named for the numbers of "John Chinamen" placering in the vicinity. It was abandoned soon after the discovery of the Comstock, although Wild Bob and Gentle Annie were still residents there when this photo was taken.

The discovery of the Gold Hill mines in 1859 practically depopulated Johntown, with many of the latter's buildings being moved intact to the new community. The founding of Virginia City a short time later led to the complete abandonment of Johntown. Gold dredges operating during the early part of the 20th century erased most signs of the early placer miners, leaving that portion of Gold Canyon strewn with now-dry ponds and mounds of gravel.

Jumbo

Located 3½ miles west of Gold Hill, a small group of previously-unknown gold and silver veins were located here in 1907. Within a year the small community established near the mines had a post office, hotel, assay office, grocery store, and a few saloons.

Even though production from the Jumbo mines was never great, one 5-stamp and two 10-stamp mills were built between 1909 and 1915. By 1921 after intermittent operations, the ore had proven too low-grade to work, the mills shut down, and Jumbo was abandoned.

Lousetown

One of the earliest transportation routes to the Comstock was the toll road from Virginia City to Stone & Gates crossing on the Truckee River east of modern Reno. Where this road from the Truckee Meadows met Lousetown Creek some nine miles north of Virginia City, a small community developed in the early 1860's as an overnight way-station for freighters.

It is believed that the original name of this settlement was Louisetown, until an early cartographer inadvertently dropped the "i." As it was a rowdy, ill-kept place, the locals are said to have felt that the name Lousetown suited them fine, and the new name was adopted.

Lousetown never consisted of more than a dozen buildings which housed a saloon, overnight accommodations, blacksmith shop, and related facilities for freight outfits and their drivers. The area did become famous for a racetrack constructed nearby, where the finest horses in the territory competed. When another track was built closer to Virginia City it retained the name Lousetown Racetrck, even though it was more than four miles from that location.

The construction of Geiger Grade in the mid-1860's and the completion of the V&T RR a few years later reduced freight traffic on this road to a trickle. Lousetown was probably abandoned prior to 1870, although horse racing continued on the Lousetown track for another decade.

Maiden Bar

A small placer mining area of this name, located 1½ miles up Gold Canyon from Chinatown and ½ mile below Johntown, was worked in the early 1850's. Late in 1853 or early the following year a combination store, saloon, and bowling alley was built here. It must have been an extremely short-lived little place, as nothing is known of Maiden Bar other than it being the site of the first recreational facility in what is now Nevada.

Mineral Rapids

Very little is known of this tiny community, originally located immediately downstream from Dayton. A 19th century historian stated, "A town was laid out here which was intended to eclipse Dayton, but did not." It must have been of some importance, however, as it had a separate post office from April, 1860, to February, 1861. Dayton soon gained prominence over all other communities in the area, and has now expanded to cover the area where Mineral Rapids once existed.

Mound House was a major transfer point between the standard gauge Virginia & Truckee RR shown entering from the southwest, and the narrow-gauge Carson & Colorado.

Mound House

The original name of this transportation community was Mound Station, established in the late 1860's as a toll-house on the Carson-Virginia City road. With the completion of the V&T RR from Virginia City to Carson in 1869, Mound House became the transfer point for all freight headed to Dayton, Sutro, and other points east and south. It was never a large or prosperous settlement during the next twelve years, suffering a decline when the Comstock boom abated in the late 1870's.

Then in April, 1881, the narrow-gauge Carson & Colorado Railroad was completed from Mound House to Hawthorne. Freight business boomed as goods and equipment bound for Aurora, Bodie, Belleville, and Candelaria had to be unloaded from the V&T's standard-gauge cars at Mound House, then reloaded on the 3-foot narrow-gauge cars of the C&C.

While Mound House remained active for the next two decades, even acquiring its own post office in 1884, the C&C did not do well. Mining throughout Nevada declined in these years, as did the number of passengers and freight shipments. Darius O. Mills, the owner of the railroad, believed he made a good deal when he sold the C&C to the Southern Pacific Railroad in 1900. However, that same year Jim Butler discovered the ore deposit which led to the founding of Tonopah, then additional strikes were made at Goldfield and Rawhide. A new mining boom occurred, with the renamed Nevada & California Railroad already there to handle the sudden demand for transportation.

Mound House was busier than ever until 1905, when the N&C's parent company felt that the time-consuming transfer of all goods from the V&T to the narrow-gauge line was untenable. A standard-gauge line was run from the SP tracks at Hazen to connect with the N&C at Churchill, then the old 3-foot tracks were widened to accept the larger cars. Mound House had been completely bypassed, with its population dwindling so rapidly that even its post office was closed the same year.

A nearby gypsum mine kept the community alive for a time until it closed in the 1920's. The removal of the V&T track from Virginia City to Carson in 1938 did away with its last reason for existence.

Ophir

The milling town of Ophir, located on the west side of Washoe Valley, was created in 1861 when the Ophir Mining Company built a 75-stamp quartz mill there. Ore from their mine in Virginia City was freighted west from the Divide over the Ophir Grade, then across a mile-long causeway built across Washoe Lake. The mill employed 165 men, boosting Ophir's population to 300 by 1863. That number of residents provided the commerce to support other businesses, making Ophir a thriving community.

The construction of the numerous quartz mills at Empire City and along the Carson River, coupled with the completion of the V&T RR, caused the town's milling business to be diverted elsewhere. By 1871 less than a hundred people remained, and by 1881 it was reported in a state of "utter desertion and demolition."

Silver City

While many historians claim that Silver City was not settled until after the discovery of the Comstock, a contemporary writer flatly stated "Silver City was settled before Virginia City." It indeed lay in the path the placer miners took working their way up to what would become Gold Hill and Virginia City. But while the Grosh brothers' cabin was located in this area as early as 1857, the community probably did not grow to any size until 1859.

Following the discovery of the Comstock, Silver City kept pace with Virginia City for a time. By 1861 it had twelve stores, four hotels, three blacksmith shops, two butcher shops, a post office, and numerous saloons serving its population in excess of 1,000.

A number of mines were opened in the immediate vicinity, as happened around every town in the region. However, Silver City was not on the main Comstock Lode and none of its mines ever became a major producer. Instead the community became a milling town, with eight reduction works containing 95 stamps being built prior to 1871. It was also an early teamsters' center, where hundreds of horses and mules were boarded while being used to haul freight and ore wagons.

But the completion of the V&T RR took away most of the freight business, as well as diverting much Comstock ore away from the town's mills to those on the Carson River. The population diminished greatly over the next few decades, although during the first twenty years of this century there were still mines and mills operating on small low-grade gold deposits.

Like Virginia City, Silver City was never completely abandoned. Today the population is again increasing, with new homes being built on the hill above the main street. A post office, one hotel, and a saloon still serve the community, while exploratory work continues in a few local mines.

Although founded earlier than Virginia City, Silver City never grew to any great size because it lacked extensive mining operations. This scene, photographed in 1862, looks up Main Street to the north with Sun Mountain in the left background. Many of the buildings visible here are still standing today, as Silver City luckily escaped destructive fires such as those which raged through other towns in the area.

Summit House

On November 29, 1861, the Nevada Territorial Legislature granted a franchise to Dr. D. M. Geiger and J. H. Tilton to construct a road from Virginia City north to the Truckee Meadows. The Geiger Grade, by which name it is still known today, was completed early in 1863 and it immediately became a well-traveled highway. One of the three stations constructed along this road was Summit House, located in a small, grassy flat four miles north of Virginia City.

This station was a popular stopping place for teamsters throughout the latter part of the 1860's until the construction of the V&T RR seriously reduced use of the road. The further dwindling of passenger and freight traffic which began a decade later hastened the station's abandonment. The paved Geiger Grade of today, constructed in 1936, passes a few hundred yards from the site of Summit House, but not even a foundation remains to mark the spot.

Washoe City as it appeared in the mid-1860's.

Sutro

When in the early 1860's Adolph Sutro hit on the idea of digging a tunnel to intersect the lower levels of the Comstock mines, he also decided to create the town of Sutro at the tunnel's mouth. Only a scattered collection of rough buildings were erected here when digging commenced in 1869, but within two years Adolph Sutro had plotted a model community.

The town of Sutro, with its parks and tree-lined streets, soon housed a population of close to 800. The residents were supplied by an assortment of stores, a church, post office, the *Sutro Independent* newspaper, a hospital, and a number of elegant homes including Sutro's own Victorian mansion.

While one of the main functions of the Sutro Tunnel was to drain hot water from the deep silver mines, another was to provide a gravity system of transportation of ore to what Sutro envisioned as a major milling center. When completed in 1878 the tunnel was used to carry off water, but the construction of the V&T RR eight years before had given the rail line an ore transportation monopoly which Sutro could not break. He left Nevada in 1880, when the town's population was down to about 400 persons. It never recovered, eventually losing its post office in 1920.

Sutro's beautiful mansion burned in 1941 and the other buildings in town were either hauled away or destroyed. Today the property is privately owned, with a few homes and outbuildings near the tunnel mouth still occupied.

Washoe City

The large mining communities along the Comstock Lode, because of their location, had to depend heavily on other towns for milling and supplies of timber and agricultural products. Wood in particular was constantly sought after. Mine engines needed it to fuel their boilers, every residence was heated by a wood stove or used one in the kitchen, most of the buildings on the Comstock were of frame construction, and the miles of underground stopes and adits were supported by wooden square-set timbering.

To aid in supplying this ceaseless demand, Washoe City came into being on the north end of Washoe Lake early in 1861. Its primary purpose was to provide timber and farm products to Virginia City, but the empty freight wagons returning from the Comstock were soon carrying ore to the 20-stamp Atchison mill. When Washoe County was created late in 1861, Washoe City became the county seat. A brick courthouse and jail were soon constructed, and by the mid-1860's this town of 6,000 was among Nevada's largest.

The flush times were short-lived, though, as the building of the V&T RR in 1869 took away much of the timber and ore milling business. Two years later

the town of Reno, which had been founded in 1868, acquired the county seat. By 1880 the number of residents numbered only 200, and 14 years later it had further shrunk to the point where a post office was no longer necessary.

By the mid-20th century Washoe City had diminished to just a few homes, although its proximity to Reno and Carson City made it inevitable that the town would develop into a satellite community. In the 1950's New Washoe City sprang up on the east side of Washoe Lake, and it now has a couple of thousand people. At the same time "old" Washoe City has again begun to grow, although only a few scattered buildings of the original city remain amid modern homes and businesses.

White Horse Station

As with Five Mile House, the exact time of the founding of this station is unknown. It is reasonable to assume that it was established around 1863, the year Dr. Geiger opened his road from the Comstock to the Truckee Meadows. Located in a narrow canyon six miles north of Virginia City, this station was also situated at the base of the steepest portion of the old grade — Deadman's Bend.

This stretch of road was well-named, as an early issue of *Nevada Highways and Parks* called it: "A road over which stage coaches with whip-cracked teams of four in the harness, bullion bars in the strong box under the high spring seats, and three or four badly shaken and frightened passengers, rattled perilously down the steep grades, brakes screeching, iron-tired wheels spitting fire while rounding the sharp, stony curves on two wheels..."

The advent of the automobile did not doom this station, as it did so many others, since drivers bound north to Reno still paused to calm their nerves after negotiating Deadman's Bend. Southbound drivers were also forced to stop for water at the station's spring, although the demand of thirsty horses for water had been replaced by that of boiling radiators.

The road's rerouting was completed in 1936, replacing the old twelve percent grade with a modern, paved highway which did not exceed six percent. Traffic on the old Geiger Grade came to a standstill, and White Horse Station was finally abandoned. The old road is still graded annually to allow access for sightseers, but not a trace is left of the station at the base of Deadman's Bend.

Index